MznLnx

Missing Links Exam Preps

Exam Prep for

Calculus Single Variable

Hughes-Hallett, Gleason, et al., 4th Edition

The MznLnx Exam Prep is your link from the texbook and lecture to your exams.
The MznLnx Exam Preps are unauthorized and comprehensive reviews of your textbooks.

All material provided by MznLnx and Rico Publications (c) 2010
Textbook publishers and textbook authors do not particpate in or contribute to these reviews.

MznLnx

Rico
Publications

Exam Prep for Calculus Single Variable
4th Edition
Hughes-Hallett, Gleason, et al.

Publisher: Raymond Houge
Assistant Editor: Michael Rouger
Text and Cover Designer: Lisa Buckner
Marketing Manager: Sara Swagger
Project Manager, Editorial Production: Jerry Emerson
Art Director: Vernon Lowerui

Product Manager: Dave Mason
Editorial Assitant: Rachel Guzmanji
Pedagogy: Debra Long
Cover Image: Jim Reed/Getty Images
Text and Cover Printer: City Printing, Inc.
Compositor: Media Mix, Inc.

(c) 2010 Rico Publications

ALL RIGHTS RESERVED. No part of this work covered by the copyright may be reproduced or used in any form or by an means--graphic, electronic, or mechanical, including photocopying, recording, taping, Web distribution, information storage, and retrieval systems, or in any other manner--without the written permission of the publisher.

Printed in the United States
ISBN:

For more information about our products, contact us at:

Dave.Mason@RicoPublications.com

For permission to use material from this text or

product, submit a request online to:

Dave.Mason@RicoPublications.com

Contents

CHAPTER 1
A LIBRARY OF FUNCTIONS   1
CHAPTER 2
KEY CONCEPT: THE DERIVATIVE   20
CHAPTER 3
SHORT-CUTS TO DIFFERENTIATION   32
CHAPTER 4
USING THE DERIVATIVE   46
CHAPTER 5
KEY CONCEPT: THE DEFINITE INTEGRAL   67
CHAPTER 6
CONSTRUCTING ANTIDERIVATIVES   77
CHAPTER 7
INTEGRATION   88
CHAPTER 8
USING THE DEFINITE INTEGRAL   104
CHAPTER 9
SEQUENCES AND SERIES   126
CHAPTER 10
APPROXIMATING FUNCTIONS USING SERIES   138
CHAPTER 11
DIFFERENTIAL EQUATIONS   142
ANSWER KEY   148

TO THE STUDENT

COMPREHENSIVE

The *MznLnx* Exam Prep series is designed to help you pass your exams. Editors at MznLnx review your textbooks and then prepare these practice exams to help you master the textbook material. Unlike study guides, workbooks, and practice tests provided by the texbook publisher and textbook authors, *MznLnx* gives you **all** of the material in each chapter in exam form, not just samples, so you can be sure to nail your exam.

MECHANICAL

The MznLnx Exam Prep series creates exams that will help you learn the subject matter as well as test you on your understanding. Each question is designed to help you master the concept. Just working through the exams, you gain an understanding of the subject--its a simple mechanical process that produces success.

INTEGRATED STUDY GUIDE AND REVIEW

MznLnx is not just a set of exams designed to test you, its also a comprehensive review of the subject content. Each exam question is also a review of the concept, making sure that you will get the answer correct without having to go to other sources of material. You learn as you go! Its the easiest way to pass an exam.

HUMOR

Studying can be tedious and dry. MznLnx's instructional design includes moderate humor within the exam questions on occassion, to break the tedium and revitalize the brain

Chapter 1. A LIBRARY OF FUNCTIONS

1. _____ is a physical property of a system that underlies the common notions of hot and cold; something that is hotter has the greater _____.
    a. Temperature0
    b. Thing
    c. Undefined
    d. Undefined

2. The mathematical concept of a _____ expresses the intuitive idea of deterministic dependence between two quantities, one of which is viewed as primary and the other as secondary. A _____ then is a way to associate a unique output for each input of a specified type, for example, a real number or an element of a given set.
    a. Function0
    b. Thing
    c. Undefined
    d. Undefined

3. A _____ is a symbolic representation denoting a quantity or expression. It often represents an "unknown" quantity that has the potential to change.
    a. Variable0
    b. Thing
    c. Undefined
    d. Undefined

4. In mathematics, the _____ of a function is the set of all "output" values produced by that function. Given a function $f : A \to B$, the _____ of f, is defined to be the set $\{x \in B : x = f(a) \text{ for some } a \in A\}$.
    a. Range0
    b. Thing
    c. Undefined
    d. Undefined

5. In mathematics, an _____ is any of the arguments, i.e. "inputs", to a function. Thus if we have a function f(x), then x is a _____.
    a. Independent variable0
    b. Thing
    c. Undefined
    d. Undefined

6. In a function the _____, is the variable which is the value, i.e. the "output", of the function.
    a. Dependent variable0
    b. Thing
    c. Undefined
    d. Undefined

7. In mathematics, a _____ of a k-place relation $L \subseteq X_1 \times \ldots \times X_k$ is one of the sets X_j, $1 \le j \le k$. In the special case where k = 2 and $L \subseteq X_1 \times X_2$ is a function $L : X_1 \to X_2$, it is conventional to refer to X_1 as the _____ of the function and to refer to X_2 as the codomain of the function.
    a. Domain0
    b. Thing
    c. Undefined
    d. Undefined

8. _____ are the basic objects of study in graph theory. Informally speaking, a graph is a set of objects called points, nodes, or vertices connected by links called lines or edges.
    a. Thing
    b. Graphs0
    c. Undefined
    d. Undefined

9. A _____ is a special kind of ratio, indicating a relationship between two measurements with different units, such as miles to gallons or cents to pounds.
    a. Thing
    b. Rate0
    c. Undefined
    d. Undefined

Chapter 1. A LIBRARY OF FUNCTIONS

10. The _____, the average in everyday English, which is also called the arithmetic _____ (and is distinguished from the geometric _____ or harmonic _____). The average is also called the sample _____. The expected value of a random variable, which is also called the population _____.
   a. Thing
   b. Mean0
   c. Undefined
   d. Undefined

11. In mathematics, a _____ may be described informally as a number that can be given by an infinite decimal representation.
   a. Thing
   b. Real number0
   c. Undefined
   d. Undefined

12. The word _____ comes from the Latin word linearis, which means created by lines.
   a. Thing
   b. Linear0
   c. Undefined
   d. Undefined

13. A _____ is a first degree polynomial mathematical function of the form: f(x) = mx + b where m and b are real constants and x is a real variable.
   a. Thing
   b. Linear function0
   c. Undefined
   d. Undefined

14. _____ is often used to describe the measurement of the steepness, incline, gradient, or grade of a straight line. The _____ is defined as the ratio of the "rise" divided by the "run" between two points on a line, or in other words, the ratio of the altitude change to the horizontal distance between any two points on the line.
   a. Slope0
   b. Thing
   c. Undefined
   d. Undefined

15. In mathematics, a _____ is a constant multiplicative factor of a certain object. The object can be such things as a variable, a vector, a function, etc. For example, the _____ of $9x^2$ is 9.
   a. Thing
   b. Coefficient0
   c. Undefined
   d. Undefined

16. Initial objects are also called _____, and terminal objects are also called final.
   a. Coterminal0
   b. Thing
   c. Undefined
   d. Undefined

17. An _____ is a straight line around which a geometric figure can be rotated.
   a. Thing
   b. Axis0
   c. Undefined
   d. Undefined

18. Any point where a graph makes contact with an coordinate axis is called an _____ of the graph
   a. Intercept0
   b. Thing
   c. Undefined
   d. Undefined

19. In mathematics and the mathematical sciences, a _____ is a fixed, but possibly unspecified, value. This is in contrast to a variable, which is not fixed.

Chapter 1. A LIBRARY OF FUNCTIONS

a. Thing
b. Constant0
c. Undefined
d. Undefined

20. _____ is a synonym for information.
    a. Data0
    b. Thing
    c. Undefined
    d. Undefined

21. A _____ function is a function for which, intuitively, small changes in the input result in small changes in the output.
    a. Continuous0
    b. Event
    c. Undefined
    d. Undefined

22. In mathematics, _____ geometry was the traditional name for the geometry of three-dimensional Euclidean space — for practical purposes the kind of space we live in.
    a. Solid0
    b. Thing
    c. Undefined
    d. Undefined

23. A _____ is a unit of length, usually used to measure distance, in a number of different systems, including Imperial units, United States customary units and Norwegian/Swedish mil. Its size can vary from system to system, but in each is between 1 and 10 kilometers. In contemporary English contexts _____ refers to either:
    a. Thing
    b. Mile0
    c. Undefined
    d. Undefined

24. In mathematics, a _____ is the end result of a division problem. It can also be expressed as the number of times the divisor divides into the dividend.
    a. Thing
    b. Quotient0
    c. Undefined
    d. Undefined

25. The function difference divided by the point difference is known as the _____
    a. Thing
    b. Difference quotient0
    c. Undefined
    d. Undefined

26. The _____ of measurement are a globally standardized and modernized form of the metric system.
    a. Units0
    b. Thing
    c. Undefined
    d. Undefined

27. In astronomy, geography, geometry and related sciences and contexts, a plane is said to be _____ at a given point if it is locally perpendicular to the gradient of the gravity field, i.e., with the direction of the gravitational force at that point.
    a. Horizontal0
    b. Thing
    c. Undefined
    d. Undefined

28. A _____ is the quantity that defines certain relatively constant characteristics of systems or functions..
    a. Thing
    b. Parameter0
    c. Undefined
    d. Undefined

Chapter 1. A LIBRARY OF FUNCTIONS

29. The _____ of a mathematical object is its size: a property by which it can be larger or smaller than other objects of the same kind; in technical terms, an ordering of the class of objects to which it belongs.
   a. Thing
   b. Magnitude0
   c. Undefined
   d. Undefined

30. In mathematics, two quantities are called _____ if they vary in such a way that one of the quantities is a constant multiple of the other, or equivalently if they have a constant ratio.
   a. Thing
   b. Proportional0
   c. Undefined
   d. Undefined

31. _____ is a special mathematical relationship between two quantities. Two quantities are called proportional if they vary in such a way that one of the quantities is a constant multiple of the other, or equivalently if they have a constant ratio.
   a. Thing
   b. Proportionality0
   c. Undefined
   d. Undefined

32. In mathematics, the term _____ is applied to certain functions. There are two common ways it is applied: these are related historically, but diverged somewhat during the twentieth century.
   a. Functional0
   b. Thing
   c. Undefined
   d. Undefined

33. In common philosophical language, a proposition or _____, is the content of an assertion, that is, it is true-or-false and defined by the meaning of a particular piece of language.
   a. Statement0
   b. Concept
   c. Undefined
   d. Undefined

34. In sociology and biology a _____ is the collection of people or organisms of a particular species living in a given geographic area or space, usually measured by a census.
   a. Population0
   b. Thing
   c. Undefined
   d. Undefined

35. In mathematics, the multiplicative inverse of a number x, denoted $1/x$ or x^{-1}, is the number which, when multiplied by x, yields 1. The multiplicative inverse of x is also called the _____ of x.
   a. Thing
   b. Reciprocal0
   c. Undefined
   d. Undefined

36. The existence and properties of _____ are the basis of Euclid's parallel postulate. _____ are two lines on the same plane that do not intersect even assuming that lines extend to infinity in either direction.
   a. Parallel lines0
   b. Thing
   c. Undefined
   d. Undefined

37. In geometry, two lines or planes if one falls on the other in such a way as to create congruent adjacent angles. The term may be used as a noun or adjective. Thus, referring to Figure 1, the line AB is the _____ to CD through the point B.
   a. Thing
   b. Perpendicular0
   c. Undefined
   d. Undefined

Chapter 1. A LIBRARY OF FUNCTIONS

38. In plane geometry, a _____ is a polygon with four equal sides, four right angles, and parallel opposite sides. In algebra, the _____ of a number is that number multiplied by itself.
   a. Thing
   b. Square0
   c. Undefined
   d. Undefined

39. A _____ is a three-dimensional solid object bounded by six square faces, facets, or sides, with three meeting at each vertex.
   a. Cube0
   b. Thing
   c. Undefined
   d. Undefined

40. _____ is a kind of property which exists as magnitude or multitude. It is among the basic classes of things along with quality, substance, change, and relation.
   a. Thing
   b. Amount0
   c. Undefined
   d. Undefined

41. _____ of an object is its speed in a particular direction.
   a. Velocity0
   b. Thing
   c. Undefined
   d. Undefined

42. _____ is a temperature scale named after the German physicist Daniel Gabriel _____ , who proposed it in 1724.
   a. Fahrenheit0
   b. Thing
   c. Undefined
   d. Undefined

43. _____ is, or relates to, the _____ temperature scale .
   a. Celsius0
   b. Thing
   c. Undefined
   d. Undefined

44. In Euclidean geometry, a _____ is the set of all points in a plane at a fixed distance, called the radius, from a given point, the center.
   a. Circle0
   b. Thing
   c. Undefined
   d. Undefined

45. In mathematics, a _____ is a two-dimensional manifold or surface that is perfectly flat.
   a. Thing
   b. Plane0
   c. Undefined
   d. Undefined

46. The _____ or kilogramme is the SI base unit of mass. It is defined as being equal to the mass of the international prototype of the _____.
   a. Kilogram0
   b. Thing
   c. Undefined
   d. Undefined

47. _____ is a term used in accounting, economics and finance with reference to the fact that assets with finite lives lose value over time.

48. In mathematics, a _____ is the result of multiplying, or an expression that identifies factors to be multiplied.
   a. Thing
   b. Product0
   c. Undefined
   d. Undefined

49. In economics, supply and _____ describe market relations between prospective sellers and buyers of a good.
   a. Demand0
   b. Thing
   c. Undefined
   d. Undefined

50. Sir Isaac _____, was an English physicist, mathematician, astronomer, natural philosopher, and alchemist, regarded by many as the greatest figure in the history of science
   a. Person
   b. Newton0
   c. Undefined
   d. Undefined

51. In mathematics, there are several meanings of _____ depending on the subject.
   a. Thing
   b. Degree0
   c. Undefined
   d. Undefined

52. An _____ of a product of sums expresses it as a sum of products by using the fact that multiplication distributes over addition.
   a. Expansion0
   b. Thing
   c. Undefined
   d. Undefined

53. In mathematics, _____ growth occurs when the growth rate of a function is always proportional to the function's current size.
   a. Thing
   b. Exponential0
   c. Undefined
   d. Undefined

54. _____ is one of the most important functions in mathematics. A function commonly used to study growth and decay
   a. Exponential function0
   b. Thing
   c. Undefined
   d. Undefined

55. _____ is change in population over time, and can be quantified as the change in the number of individuals in a population per unit time.
   a. Thing
   b. Population growth0
   c. Undefined
   d. Undefined

56. In topology and related areas of mathematics a _____ or Moore-Smith sequence is a generalization of a sequence, intended to unify the various notions of limit and generalize them to arbitrary topological spaces.
   a. Thing
   b. Net0
   c. Undefined
   d. Undefined

57. _____ is the property of a physical object that quantifies the amount of matter and energy it is equivalent to.

Chapter 1. A LIBRARY OF FUNCTIONS

a. Thing
b. Mass0
c. Undefined
d. Undefined

58. In physics, _____ is an influence that may cause an object to accelerate. It may be experienced as a lift, a push, or a pull. The actual acceleration of the body is determined by the vector sum of all forces acting on it, known as net _____ or resultant _____.
a. Force0
b. Thing
c. Undefined
d. Undefined

59. _____ is a vector produced when two or more forces act upon a single object.
a. Thing
b. Resultant force0
c. Undefined
d. Undefined

60. The plus and _____ signs are mathematical symbols used to represent the notions of positive and negative as well as the operations of addition and subtraction.
a. Thing
b. Minus0
c. Undefined
d. Undefined

61. An _____ is a combination of numbers, operators, grouping symbols and/or free variables and bound variables arranged in a meaningful way which can be evaluated..
a. Thing
b. Expression0
c. Undefined
d. Undefined

62. _____ was an Italian physicist, mathematician, astronomer, and philosopher who is closely associated with the scientific revolution.
a. Person
b. Galileo Galilei0
c. Undefined
d. Undefined

63. In mathematics, a matrix can be thought of as each row or _____ being a vector. Hence, a space formed by row vectors or _____ vectors are said to be a row space or a _____ space.
a. Column0
b. Concept
c. Undefined
d. Undefined

64. In mathematics, _____ occurs when the growth rate of a function is always proportional to the function's current size.
a. Exponential growth0
b. Thing
c. Undefined
d. Undefined

65. In mathematics, the _____ f is the collection of all ordered pairs . In particular, graph means the graphical representation of this collection, in the form of a curve or surface, together with axes, etc. Graphing on a Cartesian plane is sometimes referred to as curve sketching.
a. Graph of a function0
b. Thing
c. Undefined
d. Undefined

66. The word _____ means curving in or hollowed inward.

a. Concavity0
b. Thing
c. Undefined
d. Undefined

67. _____ is a function whose values do not vary and thus are constant.
    a. Thing
    b. Constant function0
    c. Undefined
    d. Undefined

68. _____ is a way of expressing a number as a fraction of 100 per cent meaning "per hundred".
    a. Percent0
    b. Thing
    c. Undefined
    d. Undefined

69. The _____ is the period of time required for a quantity to double in size or value.
    a. Thing
    b. Doubling time0
    c. Undefined
    d. Undefined

70. _____ is a decrease that follows an exponential function.
    a. Thing
    b. Exponential decay0
    c. Undefined
    d. Undefined

71. _____ is a mathematical subject that includes the study of limits, derivatives, integrals, and power series and constitutes a major part of modern university curriculum.
    a. Thing
    b. Calculus0
    c. Undefined
    d. Undefined

72. The _____ is the total number of human beings alive on the planet Earth at a given time.
    a. World population0
    b. Thing
    c. Undefined
    d. Undefined

73. The population _____ is the total number of human beings alive on the planet Earth at a given time.
    a. Thing
    b. Of the world0
    c. Undefined
    d. Undefined

74. In mathematics, _____ refers to the rewriting of an expression into a simpler form.
    a. Thing
    b. Reduction0
    c. Undefined
    d. Undefined

75. _____ is a business term for the amount of money that a company receives from its activities in a given period, mostly from sales of products and/or services to customers
    a. Revenue0
    b. Thing
    c. Undefined
    d. Undefined

76. In geometry, an _____ of a triangle is a straight line through a vertex and perpendicular to (i.e. forming a right angle with) the opposite side or an extension of the opposite side.
    a. Altitude0
    b. Concept
    c. Undefined
    d. Undefined

Chapter 1. A LIBRARY OF FUNCTIONS

77. In mainstream economics, the word _____ refers to a general rise in prices measured against a standard level of purchasing power.
    a. Thing
    b. Inflation0
    c. Undefined
    d. Undefined

78. A _____ is a negotiable instrument instructing a financial institution to pay a specific amount of a specific currency from a specific demand account held in the maker/depositor's name with that institution. Both the maker and payee may be natural persons or legal entities.
    a. Check0
    b. Thing
    c. Undefined
    d. Undefined

79. The _____ of a geographic location is its height above a fixed reference point, often the mean sea level.
    a. Elevation0
    b. Thing
    c. Undefined
    d. Undefined

80. In mathematics, a _____ or rhodonea curve is a sinusoid plotted in polar coordinates.
    a. Thing
    b. Rose0
    c. Undefined
    d. Undefined

81. In probability theory and statistics, a _____ is a number dividing the higher half of a sample, a population, or a probability distribution from the lower half.
    a. Median0
    b. Concept
    c. Undefined
    d. Undefined

82. A _____ of a number is the product of that number with any integer.
    a. Multiple0
    b. Thing
    c. Undefined
    d. Undefined

83. In classical geometry, a _____ of a circle or sphere is any line segment from its center to its boundary. By extension, the _____ of a circle or sphere is the length of any such segment. The _____ is half the diameter. In science and engineering the term _____ of curvature is commonly used as a synonym for _____.
    a. Thing
    b. Radius0
    c. Undefined
    d. Undefined

84. A _____ number is a positive integer which has a positive divisor other than one or itself.
    a. Composite0
    b. Thing
    c. Undefined
    d. Undefined

85. _____ has many meanings, most of which simply .
    a. Thing
    b. Power0
    c. Undefined
    d. Undefined

86. In mathematics, a _____ of a positive integer n is a way of writing n as a sum of positive integers.
    a. Composition0
    b. Thing
    c. Undefined
    d. Undefined

87. _____ means "constancy", i.e. if something retains a certain feature even after we change a way of looking at it, then it is symmetric.
   a. Symmetry0
   b. Thing
   c. Undefined
   d. Undefined

88. _____ are functions which satisfy particular symmetry relations, with respect to taking additive inverses.
   a. Thing
   b. Even function0
   c. Undefined
   d. Undefined

89. In mathematics, _____ and odd functions are functions which satisfy particular symmetry relations, with respect to taking additive inverses.
   a. Even functions0
   b. Thing
   c. Undefined
   d. Undefined

90. In mathematics, the _____ of a coordinate system is the point where the axes of the system intersect.
   a. Thing
   b. Origin0
   c. Undefined
   d. Undefined

91. In mathematics, a _____ is an expression that is constructed from one or more variables and constants, using only the operations of addition, subtraction, multiplication, and constant positive whole number exponents. is a _____. Note in particular that division by an expression containing a variable is not in general allowed in polynomials. [1]
   a. Polynomial0
   b. Thing
   c. Undefined
   d. Undefined

92. _____ element of an element x with respect to a binary operation * with identity element e is an element y such that x * y = y * x = e. In particular,
   a. Thing
   b. Inverse0
   c. Undefined
   d. Undefined

93. An _____ is a function which does the reverse of a given function.
   a. Thing
   b. Inverse function0
   c. Undefined
   d. Undefined

94. The metre (or _____, see spelling differences) is a measure of length. It is the basic unit of length in the metric system and in the International System of Units (SI), used around the world for general and scientific purposes.
   a. Meter0
   b. Concept
   c. Undefined
   d. Undefined

95. In mathematics, the idea of _____ generalises the concepts of negation, in relation to addition, and reciprocal, in relation to multiplication.
   a. Thing
   b. Inverse element0
   c. Undefined
   d. Undefined

96. _____ is a set, with some particular properties and usually some additional structure, such as the operations of addition or multiplication, for instance.

Chapter 1. A LIBRARY OF FUNCTIONS

a. Space0
b. Thing
c. Undefined
d. Undefined

97. _____ are a measure of time.
   a. Minutes0
   b. Thing
   c. Undefined
   d. Undefined

98. In mathematics, a _____ (also spelled reflexion) is a map that transforms an object into its mirror image.
   a. Reflection0
   b. Concept
   c. Undefined
   d. Undefined

99. In Euclidean geometry, a uniform _____ is a linear transformation that enlargers or diminishes objects, and whose _____ factor is the same in all directions. This is also called homothethy.
   a. Scale0
   b. Thing
   c. Undefined
   d. Undefined

100. An _____ is when two lines intersect somewhere on a plane creating a right angle at intersection
   a. Axes0
   b. Thing
   c. Undefined
   d. Undefined

101. In mathematics, an _____, mean, or central tendency of a data set refers to a measure of the "middle" or "expected" value of the data set.
   a. Average0
   b. Concept
   c. Undefined
   d. Undefined

102. In botany, _____ are above-ground plant organs specialized for photosynthesis. Their characteristics are typically analyzed by using Fiobonacci's sequences.
   a. Thing
   b. Leaves0
   c. Undefined
   d. Undefined

103. The _____ of a solid object is the three-dimensional concept of how much space it occupies, often quantified numerically.
   a. Volume0
   b. Thing
   c. Undefined
   d. Undefined

104. In mathematics, a _____ of a number x is the exponent y of the power by such that $x = b^y$. The value used for the base b must be neither 0 nor 1, nor a root of 1 in the case of the extension to complex numbers, and is typically 10, e, or 2.
   a. Logarithm0
   b. Thing
   c. Undefined
   d. Undefined

105. _____ is the logarithm to the base e, where e is an irrational constant approximately equal to 2.718281828459.
   a. Natural logarithm0
   b. Thing
   c. Undefined
   d. Undefined

106. _____ is a straight line or curve A to which another curve B the one being studied approaches closer and closer as one moves along it.

Chapter 1. A LIBRARY OF FUNCTIONS

a. Vertical asymptote0
b. Thing
c. Undefined
d. Undefined

107. An _____ is a straight line or curve A to which another curve B approaches closer and closer as one moves along it. As one moves along B, the space between it and the _____ A becomes smaller and smaller, and can in fact be made as small as one could wish by going far enough along. A curve may or may not touch or cross its _____. In fact, the curve may intersect the _____ an infinite number of times.
a. Asymptote0
b. Thing
c. Undefined
d. Undefined

108. A _____ is a function that assigns a number to subsets of a given set.
a. Thing
b. Measure0
c. Undefined
d. Undefined

109. A _____ is a deliberate process for transforming one or more inputs into one or more results.
a. Calculation0
b. Thing
c. Undefined
d. Undefined

110. _____ is the level of functional and/or metabolic efficiency of an organism at both the micro level.
a. Thing
b. Health0
c. Undefined
d. Undefined

111. A _____ is one of the basic shapes of geometry: a polygon with three vertices and three sides which are straight line segments.
a. Thing
b. Triangle0
c. Undefined
d. Undefined

112. In mathematics, the _____ functions are functions of an angle; they are important when studying triangles and modeling periodic phenomena, among many other applications.
a. Thing
b. Trigonometric0
c. Undefined
d. Undefined

113. The _____ are functions of an angle; they are important when studying triangles and modeling periodic phenomena, among many other applications.
a. Thing
b. Trigonometric functions0
c. Undefined
d. Undefined

114. _____ is a branch of mathematics which deals with triangles, particularly triangles in a plane where one angle of the triangle is 90 degrees, and a variety of other topological relations such as spheres, in other branches, such as spherical _____.
a. Trigonometry0
b. Thing
c. Undefined
d. Undefined

115. _____ is the estimation of a physical quantity such as distance, energy, temperature, or time.

a. Measurement0   b. Thing
c. Undefined   d. Undefined

116. The _____ is a unit of plane angle. It is represented by the symbol "rad" or, more rarely, by the superscript c (for "circular measure"). For example, an angle of 1.2 radians would be written "1.2 rad" or "1.2c" (second symbol can produce confusion with centigrads).
   a. Radian0   b. Thing
   c. Undefined   d. Undefined

117. In Euclidean geometry, an _____ is a closed segment of a differentiable curve in the two-dimensional plane; for example, a circular _____ is a segment of a circle.
   a. Concept   b. Arc0
   c. Undefined   d. Undefined

118. _____ is a circle with a unit radius, i.e., a circle whose radius is 1.
   a. Thing   b. Unit circle0
   c. Undefined   d. Undefined

119. In geometry, the _____ of an object is a point in some sense in the middle of the object.
   a. Thing   b. Center0
   c. Undefined   d. Undefined

120. A _____ is a movement of an object in a circular motion. A two-dimensional object rotates around a center (or point) of _____. A three-dimensional object rotates around a line called an axis. If the axis of _____ is within the body, the body is said to rotate upon itself, or spin—which implies relative speed and perhaps free-movement with angular momentum. A circular motion about an external point, e.g. the Earth about the Sun, is called an orbit or more properly an orbital revolution.
   a. Rotation0   b. Thing
   c. Undefined   d. Undefined

121. The _____ is the distance around a closed curve. _____ is a kind of perimeter.
   a. Circumference0   b. Thing
   c. Undefined   d. Undefined

122. _____ is a trigonemtric function that is important when studying triangles and modeling periodic phenomena, among other applications.
   a. Thing   b. Sine0
   c. Undefined   d. Undefined

123. A _____ is a set of numbers that designate location in a given reference system, such as x,y in a planar _____ system or an x,y,z in a three-dimensional _____ system.
   a. Coordinate0   b. Thing
   c. Undefined   d. Undefined

124. The _____ of an angle is the ratio of the length of the adjacent side to the length of the hypotenuse.

a. Concept
b. Cosine0
c. Undefined
d. Undefined

125. In business, particularly accounting, a _____ is the time intervals that the accounts, statement, payments, or other calculations cover.
   a. Thing
   b. Period0
   c. Undefined
   d. Undefined

126. The _____ is a nonnegative scalar measure of a wave's magnitude of oscillation, that is, the magnitude of the maximum disturbance in the medium during one wave cycle.
   a. Thing
   b. Amplitude0
   c. Undefined
   d. Undefined

127. In mathematics, the concept of a _____ tries to capture the intuitive idea of a geometrical one-dimensional and continuous object. A simple example is the circle.
   a. Curve0
   b. Thing
   c. Undefined
   d. Undefined

128. _____ are the cyclic rizing and falling of Earth's ocean surface caused by the tidal forces of the Moon and the sun acting on the oceans.
   a. Thing
   b. Tides0
   c. Undefined
   d. Undefined

129. In elementary algebra, an _____ is a set that contains every real number between two indicated numbers and may contain the two numbers themselves.
   a. Thing
   b. Interval0
   c. Undefined
   d. Undefined

130. In trigonometry, the _____ is a function defined as $\tan x = \sin x / \cos x$. The function is so-named because it can be defined as the length of a certain segment of a _____ (in the geometric sense) to the unit circle. In plane geometry, a line is _____ to a curve, at some point, if both line and curve pass through the point with the same direction.
   a. Tangent0
   b. Thing
   c. Undefined
   d. Undefined

131. In mathematics, the _____ are the inverse functions of the trigonometric functions.
   a. Thing
   b. Inverse trigonometric functions0
   c. Undefined
   d. Undefined

132. A _____ given two distinct points A and B on the _____, is the set of points C on the line containing points A and B such that A is not strictly between C and B.
   a. Ray0
   b. Thing
   c. Undefined
   d. Undefined

133. In mathematics, defined and _____ are used to explain whether or not expressions have meaningful, sensible, and unambiguous values.

Chapter 1. A LIBRARY OF FUNCTIONS

a. Thing
b. Undefined0
c. Undefined
d. Undefined

134. In mathematics, a subset of Euclidean space R^n is called _____ if it is closed and bounded.
   a. Thing
   b. Compact0
   c. Undefined
   d. Undefined

135. Equivalence is the condition of being _____ or essentially equal.
   a. Thing
   b. Equivalent0
   c. Undefined
   d. Undefined

136. _____ means in succession or back-to-back
   a. Consecutive0
   b. Thing
   c. Undefined
   d. Undefined

137. In economics, economic _____ is simply a state of the world where economic forces are balanced and in the absence of external influences the values of economic variables will not change.
   a. Equilibrium0
   b. Thing
   c. Undefined
   d. Undefined

138. _____ is the difference of electrical potential between two points of an electrical or electronic circuit, expressed in volts
   a. Thing
   b. Voltage0
   c. Undefined
   d. Undefined

139. _____ is defined as the rate of change or derivative with respect to time of velocity.
   a. Acceleration0
   b. Thing
   c. Undefined
   d. Undefined

140. In mathematics, a _____ number is a number which can be expressed as a ratio of two integers. Non-integer _____ numbers (commonly called fractions) are usually written as the vulgar fraction a / b, where b is not zero.
   a. Thing
   b. Rational0
   c. Undefined
   d. Undefined

141. In mathematics, a _____ is any function which can be written as the ratio of two polynomial functions.
   a. Thing
   b. Rational function0
   c. Undefined
   d. Undefined

142. The _____ integers are all the integers from zero on upwards.
   a. Thing
   b. Nonnegative0
   c. Undefined
   d. Undefined

143. A _____ is the result of the addition of a set of numbers. The numbers may be natural numbers, complex numbers, matrices, or still more complicated objects. An infinite _____ is a subtle procedure known as a series.

Chapter 1. A LIBRARY OF FUNCTIONS

    a. Thing   b. Sum0
    c. Undefined   d. Undefined

144. _____ is a mathematical operation, written a^n, involving two numbers, the base a and the exponent n.
    a. Exponentiating0   b. Thing
    c. Undefined   d. Undefined

145. _____ is a mathematical operation, written a^n, involving two numbers, the base a and the exponent n.
    a. Exponentiation0   b. Thing
    c. Undefined   d. Undefined

146. A _____ is 360° or 2∂ radians.
    a. Turn0   b. Thing
    c. Undefined   d. Undefined

147. In mathematics, the _____ is a conic section generated by the intersection of a right circular conical surface and a plane parallel to a generating straight line of that surface. It can also be defined as locus of points in a plane which are equidistant from a given point.
    a. Thing   b. Parabola0
    c. Undefined   d. Undefined

148. In mathematics, factorization (British English: factorisation) or factoring is the decomposition of an object (for example, a number, a polynomial, or a matrix) into a product of other objects, or _____, which when multiplied together give the original.
    a. Thing   b. Factors0
    c. Undefined   d. Undefined

149. A _____ is the part of a fraction that tells how many equal parts make up a whole, and which is used in the name of the fraction: "halves", "thirds", "fourths" or "quarters", "fifths" and so on.
    a. Denominator0   b. Concept
    c. Undefined   d. Undefined

150. In mathematics, a set is called _____ if there is a bijection between the set and some set of the form {1, 2, ..., n} where n is a natural number.
    a. Thing   b. Finite0
    c. Undefined   d. Undefined

151. A _____ is a polynomial function of the form $f(x) = ax^2 + bx + c$, where a, b, c are real numbers and a ≠ 0.
    a. Event   b. Quadratic function0
    c. Undefined   d. Undefined

152. In mathematics, a _____ is a statement that can be proved on the basis of explicitly stated or previously agreed assumptions.
    a. Theorem0   b. Thing
    c. Undefined   d. Undefined

Chapter 1. A LIBRARY OF FUNCTIONS

153. The _____ implies that on any great circle around the world, the temperature, pressure, elevation, carbon dioxide concentration, or anything else that varies continuously, there will always exist two antipodal points that share the same value for that variable.
   a. Intermediate Value Theorem0
   b. Thing
   c. Undefined
   d. Undefined

154. Mathematical _____ is used to represent ideas.
   a. Thing
   b. Notation0
   c. Undefined
   d. Undefined

155. In a mathematical proof or a syllogism, a _____ is a statement that is the logical consequence of preceding statements.
   a. Concept
   b. Conclusion0
   c. Undefined
   d. Undefined

156. _____ was a French mathematician. He started the project of formulating and proving the theorems of calculus in a rigorous manner and was thus an early pioneer of analysis. He also gave several important theorems in complex analysis and initiated the study of permutation groups. A profound mathematician, he exercised by his perspicuous and rigorous methods a great influence over his contemporaries and successors. His writings cover the entire range of mathematics and mathematical physics.
   a. Person
   b. Augustin Louis Cauchy0
   c. Undefined
   d. Undefined

157. In mathematics, science including computer science, linguistics and engineering, an _____ is, generally speaking, an independent variable or input to a function.
   a. Thing
   b. Argument0
   c. Undefined
   d. Undefined

158. In mathematics, the _____ (or modulus) of a real number is its numerical value without regard to its sign.
   a. Thing
   b. Absolute value0
   c. Undefined
   d. Undefined

159. _____ is the state of being greater than any finite number, however large.
   a. Infinity0
   b. Thing
   c. Undefined
   d. Undefined

160. In mathematics, a _____ is a demonstration that, assuming certain axioms, some statement is necessarily true.
   a. Thing
   b. Proof0
   c. Undefined
   d. Undefined

161. _____ is a branch of mathematics concerning the study of structure, relation and quantity.
   a. Algebra0
   b. Concept
   c. Undefined
   d. Undefined

162. An _____ or member of a set is an object that when collected together make up the set.

Chapter 1. A LIBRARY OF FUNCTIONS

a. Thing
b. Element0
c. Undefined
d. Undefined

163. When _____ symmetry one can determine whether or not an object is symmetric with respect to a given mathematical operation, if, when applied to the object, this operation does not change the object or its appearance.
a. Investigating0
b. Thing
c. Undefined
d. Undefined

164. In physics, an _____ is the path that an object makes around another object while under the influence of a source of centripetal force, such as gravity.
a. Thing
b. Orbit0
c. Undefined
d. Undefined

165. A _____, as defined by the International Astronomical Union, is a celestial body orbiting a star or stellar remnant that is massive enough to be rounded by its own gravity, not massive enough to cause thermonuclear fusion in its core, and has cleared its neighboring region of planetesimals.
a. Planet0
b. Thing
c. Undefined
d. Undefined

166. _____ was a German Lutheran mathematician, astronomer and astrologer, and a key figure in the 17th century astronomical revolution.
a. Person
b. Johannes Kepler0
c. Undefined
d. Undefined

167. The _____ of an algebraic expression is the same equation, but without parentheses.
a. Thing
b. Expanded form0
c. Undefined
d. Undefined

168. The deductive-nomological model is a formalized view of scientific _____ in natural language.
a. Thing
b. Explanation0
c. Undefined
d. Undefined

169. A _____ is a function that repeats its values after some definite period has been added to its independent variable.
a. Periodic function0
b. Thing
c. Undefined
d. Undefined

170. In logic, and especially in its applications to mathematics and philosophy, a _____ is an exception to a proposed general rule, i.e., a specific instance of the falsity of a universal quantification (a "for all" statement).
a. Thing
b. Counterexample0
c. Undefined
d. Undefined

171. A _____ is a quantity that denotes the proportional amount or magnitude of one quantity relative to another.
a. Thing
b. Ratio0
c. Undefined
d. Undefined

172. A _____ is a type of debt. All material things can be lent but this article focuses exclusively on monetary loans. Like all debt instruments, a _____ entails the redistribution of financial assets over time, between the lender and the borrower.
   a. Loan0
   c. Undefined
   b. Thing
   d. Undefined

173. _____ is the fee paid on borrowed money.
   a. Interest0
   c. Undefined
   b. Thing
   d. Undefined

174. The _____ is a measurement of how a function changes when the values of its inputs change.
   a. Thing
   c. Undefined
   b. Derivative0
   d. Undefined

Chapter 2. KEY CONCEPT: THE DERIVATIVE

1. Sir Isaac _____, was an English physicist, mathematician, astronomer, natural philosopher, and alchemist, regarded by many as the greatest figure in the history of science
   a. Person
   b. Newton0
   c. Undefined
   d. Undefined

2. _____ is an adjective usually refering to being in the centre.
   a. Central0
   b. Thing
   c. Undefined
   d. Undefined

3. _____ is a mathematical subject that includes the study of limits, derivatives, integrals, and power series and constitutes a major part of modern university curriculum.
   a. Calculus0
   b. Thing
   c. Undefined
   d. Undefined

4. In elementary algebra, an _____ is a set that contains every real number between two indicated numbers and may contain the two numbers themselves.
   a. Thing
   b. Interval0
   c. Undefined
   d. Undefined

5. _____ is the estimation of a physical quantity such as distance, energy, temperature, or time.
   a. Measurement0
   b. Thing
   c. Undefined
   d. Undefined

6. _____ of an object is its speed in a particular direction.
   a. Thing
   b. Velocity0
   c. Undefined
   d. Undefined

7. In mathematics, an _____, mean, or central tendency of a data set refers to a measure of the "middle" or "expected" value of the data set.
   a. Concept
   b. Average0
   c. Undefined
   d. Undefined

8. In the scientific method, an _____ (Latin: ex-+-periri, "of (or from) trying"), is a set of actions and observations, performed in the context of solving a particular problem or question, in order to support or falsify a hypothesis or research concerning phenomena.
   a. Thing
   b. Experiment0
   c. Undefined
   d. Undefined

9. _____ is the transport of people on a trip/journey or the process or time involved in a person or object moving from one location to another.
   a. Thing
   b. Travel0
   c. Undefined
   d. Undefined

10. The _____ of a mathematical object is its size: a property by which it can be larger or smaller than other objects of the same kind; in technical terms, an ordering of the class of objects to which it belongs.

Chapter 2. KEY CONCEPT: THE DERIVATIVE

    a. Thing
    b. Magnitude0
    c. Undefined
    d. Undefined

11. In topology and related areas of mathematics a _____ or Moore-Smith sequence is a generalization of a sequence, intended to unify the various notions of limit and generalize them to arbitrary topological spaces.
    a. Net0
    b. Thing
    c. Undefined
    d. Undefined

12. The _____, the average in everyday English, which is also called the arithmetic _____ (and is distinguished from the geometric _____ or harmonic _____). The average is also called the sample _____. The expected value of a random variable, which is also called the population _____.
    a. Thing
    b. Mean0
    c. Undefined
    d. Undefined

13. _____ is a synonym for information.
    a. Thing
    b. Data0
    c. Undefined
    d. Undefined

14. A _____ is 360° or 2δ radians.
    a. Thing
    b. Turn0
    c. Undefined
    d. Undefined

15. Mathematical _____ is used to represent ideas.
    a. Notation0
    b. Thing
    c. Undefined
    d. Undefined

16. The _____ is a measurement of how a function changes when the values of its inputs change.
    a. Thing
    b. Derivative0
    c. Undefined
    d. Undefined

17. In mathematics, science including computer science, linguistics and engineering, an _____ is, generally speaking, an independent variable or input to a function.
    a. Argument0
    b. Thing
    c. Undefined
    d. Undefined

18. _____ is often used to describe the measurement of the steepness, incline, gradient, or grade of a straight line. The _____ is defined as the ratio of the "rise" divided by the "run" between two points on a line, or in other words, the ratio of the altitude change to the horizontal distance between any two points on the line.
    a. Slope0
    b. Thing
    c. Undefined
    d. Undefined

19. In mathematics, the concept of a _____ tries to capture the intuitive idea of a geometrical one-dimensional and continuous object. A simple example is the circle.
    a. Thing
    b. Curve0
    c. Undefined
    d. Undefined

Chapter 2. KEY CONCEPT: THE DERIVATIVE

20. In Euclidean geometry, a uniform _____ is a linear transformation that enlargers or diminishes objects, and whose _____ factor is the same in all directions. This is also called homothethy.
    a. Thing
    b. Scale0
    c. Undefined
    d. Undefined

21. The mathematical concept of a _____ expresses the intuitive idea of deterministic dependence between two quantities, one of which is viewed as primary and the other as secondary. A _____ then is a way to associate a unique output for each input of a specified type, for example, a real number or an element of a given set.
    a. Thing
    b. Function0
    c. Undefined
    d. Undefined

22. In mathematics, the _____ f is the collection of all ordered pairs . In particular, graph means the graphical representation of this collection, in the form of a curve or surface, together with axes, etc. Graphing on a Cartesian plane is sometimes referred to as curve sketching.
    a. Thing
    b. Graph of a function0
    c. Undefined
    d. Undefined

23. The act of _____ is the calculated approximation of a result which is usable even if input data may be incomplete, uncertain, or noisy.
    a. Thing
    b. Estimating0
    c. Undefined
    d. Undefined

24. The word _____ comes from the Latin word linearis, which means created by lines.
    a. Thing
    b. Linear0
    c. Undefined
    d. Undefined

25. _____ is a branch of mathematics concerning the study of structure, relation and quantity.
    a. Algebra0
    b. Concept
    c. Undefined
    d. Undefined

26. The metre (or _____, see spelling differences) is a measure of length. It is the basic unit of length in the metric system and in the International System of Units (SI), used around the world for general and scientific purposes.
    a. Concept
    b. Meter0
    c. Undefined
    d. Undefined

27. In mathematics and the mathematical sciences, a _____ is a fixed, but possibly unspecified, value. This is in contrast to a variable, which is not fixed.
    a. Constant0
    b. Thing
    c. Undefined
    d. Undefined

28. In mathematics, a _____ is the end result of a division problem. It can also be expressed as the number of times the divisor divides into the dividend.
    a. Quotient0
    b. Thing
    c. Undefined
    d. Undefined

Chapter 2. KEY CONCEPT: THE DERIVATIVE

29. A _____ is a special kind of ratio, indicating a relationship between two measurements with different units, such as miles to gallons or cents to pounds.
    a. Rate0
    b. Thing
    c. Undefined
    d. Undefined

30. A _____ is a quantity that denotes the proportional amount or magnitude of one quantity relative to another.
    a. Ratio0
    b. Thing
    c. Undefined
    d. Undefined

31. The function difference divided by the point difference is known as the _____
    a. Thing
    b. Difference quotient0
    c. Undefined
    d. Undefined

32. A _____ is a symbolic representation denoting a quantity or expression. It often represents an "unknown" quantity that has the potential to change.
    a. Thing
    b. Variable0
    c. Undefined
    d. Undefined

33. In mathematics, an _____ is any of the arguments, i.e. "inputs", to a function. Thus if we have a function f(x), then x is a _____.
    a. Independent variable0
    b. Thing
    c. Undefined
    d. Undefined

34. _____ is a form of periodic payment from an employer to an employee, which is specified in an employment contract.
    a. Thing
    b. Gross pay0
    c. Undefined
    d. Undefined

35. A _____ is a form of periodic payment from an employer to an employee, which is specified in an employment contract.
    a. Thing
    b. Salary0
    c. Undefined
    d. Undefined

36. The _____ of a solid object is the three-dimensional concept of how much space it occupies, often quantified numerically.
    a. Thing
    b. Volume0
    c. Undefined
    d. Undefined

37. In classical geometry, a _____ of a circle or sphere is any line segment from its center to its boundary. By extension, the _____ of a circle or sphere is the length of any such segment. The _____ is half the diameter. In science and engineering the term _____ of curvature is commonly used as a synonym for _____.
    a. Thing
    b. Radius0
    c. Undefined
    d. Undefined

Chapter 2. KEY CONCEPT: THE DERIVATIVE

38. In mathematics, a _____ is the set of all points in three-dimensional space (R^3) which are at distance r from a fixed point of that space, where r is a positive real number called the radius of the _____. The fixed point is called the center or centre, and is not part of the _____ itself.
    a. Thing
    b. Sphere0
    c. Undefined
    d. Undefined

39. In trigonometry, the _____ is a function defined as tan x = $\sin x / \cos x$. The function is so-named because it can be defined as the length of a certain segment of a _____ (in the geometric sense) to the unit circle. In plane geometry, a line is _____ to a curve, at some point, if both line and curve pass through the point with the same direction.
    a. Thing
    b. Tangent0
    c. Undefined
    d. Undefined

40. The _____ is a unit of plane angle. It is represented by the symbol "rad" or, more rarely, by the superscript c (for "circular measure"). For example, an angle of 1.2 radians would be written "1.2 rad" or "1.2c" (second symbol can produce confusion with centigrads).
    a. Thing
    b. Radian0
    c. Undefined
    d. Undefined

41. _____ has two distinct but etymologically-related meanings: one in geometry and one in trigonometry.
    a. Tangent line0
    b. Thing
    c. Undefined
    d. Undefined

42. _____ is a trigonemtric function that is important when studying triangles and modeling periodic phenomena, among other applications.
    a. Thing
    b. Sine0
    c. Undefined
    d. Undefined

43. _____ are the basic objects of study in graph theory. Informally speaking, a graph is a set of objects called points, nodes, or vertices connected by links called lines or edges.
    a. Graphs0
    b. Thing
    c. Undefined
    d. Undefined

44. In mathematics, there are several meanings of _____ depending on the subject.
    a. Degree0
    b. Thing
    c. Undefined
    d. Undefined

45. In mathematics, _____ growth occurs when the growth rate of a function is always proportional to the function's current size.
    a. Thing
    b. Exponential0
    c. Undefined
    d. Undefined

46. _____ is one of the most important functions in mathematics. A function commonly used to study growth and decay
    a. Exponential function0
    b. Thing
    c. Undefined
    d. Undefined

Chapter 2. KEY CONCEPT: THE DERIVATIVE

47. The word _____ means curving in or hollowed inward.
    a. Concavity0
    b. Thing
    c. Undefined
    d. Undefined

48. Deductive _____ is the kind of _____ in which the conclusion is necessitated by, or reached from, previously known facts (the premises).
    a. Thing
    b. Reasoning0
    c. Undefined
    d. Undefined

49. An _____ is when two lines intersect somewhere on a plane creating a right angle at intersection
    a. Axes0
    b. Thing
    c. Undefined
    d. Undefined

50. A _____ is the part of a fraction that tells how many equal parts make up a whole, and which is used in the name of the fraction: "halves", "thirds", "fourths" or "quarters", "fifths" and so on.
    a. Denominator0
    b. Concept
    c. Undefined
    d. Undefined

51. In plane geometry, a _____ is a polygon with four equal sides, four right angles, and parallel opposite sides. In algebra, the _____ of a number is that number multiplied by itself.
    a. Square0
    b. Thing
    c. Undefined
    d. Undefined

52. A _____ is a tool similar to a ruler, but without markings.
    a. Straightedge0
    b. Thing
    c. Undefined
    d. Undefined

53. In mathematics, a _____ of a k-place relation $L \subseteq X_1 \times ... \times X_k$ is one of the sets X_j, $1 \leq j \leq k$. In the special case where k = 2 and $L \subseteq X_1 \times X_2$ is a function $L : X_1 \to X_2$, it is conventional to refer to X_1 as the _____ of the function and to refer to X_2 as the codomain of the function.
    a. Thing
    b. Domain0
    c. Undefined
    d. Undefined

54. In astronomy, geography, geometry and related sciences and contexts, a plane is said to be _____ at a given point if it is locally perpendicular to the gradient of the gravity field, i.e., with the direction of the gravitational force at that point.
    a. Horizontal0
    b. Thing
    c. Undefined
    d. Undefined

55. A _____ is a first degree polynomial mathematical function of the form: f(x) = mx + b where m and b are real constants and x is a real variable.
    a. Linear function0
    b. Thing
    c. Undefined
    d. Undefined

56. _____ is a function whose values do not vary and thus are constant.

a. Thing	b. Constant function0
c. Undefined	d. Undefined

57. An _____ is a combination of numbers, operators, grouping symbols and/or free variables and bound variables arranged in a meaningful way which can be evaluated..
   a. Thing	b. Expression0
   c. Undefined	d. Undefined

58. _____ is the difference of electrical potential between two points of an electrical or electronic circuit, expressed in volts
   a. Voltage0	b. Thing
   c. Undefined	d. Undefined

59. In mathematics, two quantities are called _____ if they vary in such a way that one of the quantities is a constant multiple of the other, or equivalently if they have a constant ratio.
   a. Proportional0	b. Thing
   c. Undefined	d. Undefined

60. _____ is a special mathematical relationship between two quantities.Two quantities are called proportional if they vary in such a way that one of the quantities is a constant multiple of the other, or equivalently if they have a constant ratio.
   a. Proportionality0	b. Thing
   c. Undefined	d. Undefined

61. A _____ is a large group of animals. The term is usually applied to mammals, particularly ungulates. Other terms are used for similar phenomena in other types of animal.
   a. Herd0	b. Thing
   c. Undefined	d. Undefined

62. In sociology and biology a _____ is the collection of people or organisms of a particular species living in a given geographic area or space, usually measured by a census.
   a. Population0	b. Thing
   c. Undefined	d. Undefined

63. The _____ of measurement are a globally standardized and modernized form of the metric system.
   a. Thing	b. Units0
   c. Undefined	d. Undefined

64. _____ was a German mathematician and philosopher. He invented calculus independently of Newton, and his notation is the one in general use since.
   a. Leibniz0	b. Person
   c. Undefined	d. Undefined

65. _____ is the change in total cost that arises when the quantity produced changes by one unit.

Chapter 2. KEY CONCEPT: THE DERIVATIVE

a. Marginal cost0
b. Thing
c. Undefined
d. Undefined

66. In common philosophical language, a proposition or _____, is the content of an assertion, that is, it is true-or-false and defined by the meaning of a particular piece of language.
   a. Statement0
   b. Concept
   c. Undefined
   d. Undefined

67. _____ is, or relates to, the _____ temperature scale .
   a. Celsius0
   b. Thing
   c. Undefined
   d. Undefined

68. _____ is a physical property of a system that underlies the common notions of hot and cold; something that is hotter has the greater _____.
   a. Thing
   b. Temperature0
   c. Undefined
   d. Undefined

69. _____ are a measure of time.
   a. Thing
   b. Minutes0
   c. Undefined
   d. Undefined

70. _____ is a temperature scale named after the German physicist Daniel Gabriel _____ , who proposed it in 1724.
   a. Fahrenheit0
   b. Thing
   c. Undefined
   d. Undefined

71. When _____ symmetry one can determine whether or not an object is symmetric with respect to a given mathematical operation, if, when applied to the object, this operation does not change the object or its appearance.
   a. Investigating0
   b. Thing
   c. Undefined
   d. Undefined

72. The _____ of a geographic location is its height above a fixed reference point, often the mean sea level.
   a. Elevation0
   b. Thing
   c. Undefined
   d. Undefined

73. A _____ is a unit of length, usually used to measure distance, in a number of different systems, including Imperial units, United States customary units and Norwegian/Swedish mil. Its size can vary from system to system, but in each is between 1 and 10 kilometers. In contemporary English contexts _____ refers to either:
   a. Thing
   b. Mile0
   c. Undefined
   d. Undefined

74. In mathematics, _____ refers to the rewriting of an expression into a simpler form.
   a. Thing
   b. Reduction0
   c. Undefined
   d. Undefined

Chapter 2. KEY CONCEPT: THE DERIVATIVE

75. _____ Any process by which a specified characteristic usually amplitude of the output of a device is prevented from exceeding a predetermined value.
  a. Limiting0
  b. Thing
  c. Undefined
  d. Undefined

76. _____ is the ability to hold, receive or absorb, or a measure thereof, similar to the concept of volume.
  a. Capacity0
  b. Concept
  c. Undefined
  d. Undefined

77. _____ usually refers to the biological _____ of a population level that can be supported for an organism, given the quantity of food, habitat, water and other life infrastructure present.
  a. Carrying capacity0
  b. Thing
  c. Undefined
  d. Undefined

78. In business, particularly accounting, a _____ is the time intervals that the accounts, statement, payments, or other calculations cover.
  a. Period0
  b. Thing
  c. Undefined
  d. Undefined

79. _____ is defined as the rate of change or derivative with respect to time of velocity.
  a. Acceleration0
  b. Thing
  c. Undefined
  d. Undefined

80. _____ is the design, analysis, and/or construction of works for practical purposes.
  a. Engineering0
  b. Thing
  c. Undefined
  d. Undefined

81. A _____ function is a function for which, intuitively, small changes in the input result in small changes in the output.
  a. Continuous0
  b. Event
  c. Undefined
  d. Undefined

82. A _____ is a number that is less than zero.
  a. Thing
  b. Negative number0
  c. Undefined
  d. Undefined

83. In mathematics, a _____ is a statement that can be proved on the basis of explicitly stated or previously agreed assumptions.
  a. Thing
  b. Theorem0
  c. Undefined
  d. Undefined

84. In mathematics, defined and _____ are used to explain whether or not expressions have meaningful, sensible, and unambiguous values.
  a. Undefined0
  b. Thing
  c. Undefined
  d. Undefined

85. In geometry, the _____ of an object is a point in some sense in the middle of the object.
   a. Thing
   b. Center0
   c. Undefined
   d. Undefined

86. In mathematics, a _____ is a quadric surface, with the following equation in Cartesian coordinates: $(x/_a)^2 + (y/_b)^2 = 1$.
   a. Thing
   b. Cylinder0
   c. Undefined
   d. Undefined

87. In physics, a _____ may refer to the scalar _____ or to the vector _____.
   a. Potential0
   b. Thing
   c. Undefined
   d. Undefined

88. In mathematical analysis, _____ are objects which generalize functions and probability distributions.
   a. Distribution0
   b. Thing
   c. Undefined
   d. Undefined

89. _____ has many meanings, most of which simply .
   a. Power0
   b. Thing
   c. Undefined
   d. Undefined

90. In geographic information systems, a _____ comprises an entity with a geographic location, typically determined by points, arcs, or polygons. Carriageways and cadastres exemplify _____ data.
   a. Thing
   b. Feature0
   c. Undefined
   d. Undefined

91. A _____ is a numeral used to indicate a count. The most common use of the word today is to name the part of a fraction that tells the number or count of equal parts.
   a. Numerator0
   b. Thing
   c. Undefined
   d. Undefined

92. An _____ is an increase, either of some fixed amount, for example added regularly, or of a variable amount.
   a. Thing
   b. Increment0
   c. Undefined
   d. Undefined

93. In Euclidean geometry, a _____ is the set of all points in a plane at a fixed distance, called the radius, from a given point, the center.
   a. Circle0
   b. Thing
   c. Undefined
   d. Undefined

94. In mathematics, the _____ of a coordinate system is the point where the axes of the system intersect.
   a. Origin0
   b. Thing
   c. Undefined
   d. Undefined

95. _____ means "constancy", i.e. if something retains a certain feature even after we change a way of looking at it, then it is symmetric.

Chapter 2. KEY CONCEPT: THE DERIVATIVE

a. Thing
b. Symmetry0
c. Undefined
d. Undefined

96. _____ is a unit of speed, expressing the number of international miles covered per hour.
a. Thing
b. Miles per hour0
c. Undefined
d. Undefined

97. In mathematics, a _____ of a number x is the exponent y of the power by such that $x = b^y$. The value used for the base b must be neither 0 nor 1, nor a root of 1 in the case of the extension to complex numbers, and is typically 10, e, or 2.
a. Thing
b. Logarithm0
c. Undefined
d. Undefined

98. In mathematics, a _____ is a mathematical statement which appears likely to be true, but has not been formally proven to be true under the rules of mathematical logic.
a. Concept
b. Conjecture0
c. Undefined
d. Undefined

99. A _____ is a negotiable instrument instructing a financial institution to pay a specific amount of a specific currency from a specific demand account held in the maker/depositor's name with that institution. Both the maker and payee may be natural persons or legal entities.
a. Check0
b. Thing
c. Undefined
d. Undefined

100. In mathematics, a _____ is the result of multiplying, or an expression that identifies factors to be multiplied.
a. Product0
b. Thing
c. Undefined
d. Undefined

101. In statistics, a _____ measure is one which is measuring what is supposed to measure.
a. Valid0
b. Thing
c. Undefined
d. Undefined

102. In logic, and especially in its applications to mathematics and philosophy, a _____ is an exception to a proposed general rule, i.e., a specific instance of the falsity of a universal quantification (a "for all" statement).
a. Counterexample0
b. Thing
c. Undefined
d. Undefined

103. _____, usually denoted symbolically by the Greek letter phi, Î¦, gives the location of a place on Earth north or south of the equator. _____ is an angular measurement in degrees (marked with Â°) ranging from 0Â° at the Equator (low _____) to 90Â° at the poles (90Â° N for the North Pole or 90Â° S for the South Pole; high _____). The complementary angle of a _____ is called the colatitude.
a. Latitude0
b. Thing
c. Undefined
d. Undefined

104. In mathematical analysis, a _____ is a classification of functions according to the properties of their derivatives.

a. Thing
b. Smooth surface0
c. Undefined
d. Undefined

Chapter 3. SHORT-CUTS TO DIFFERENTIATION

1. _____ is often used to describe the measurement of the steepness, incline, gradient, or grade of a straight line. The _____ is defined as the ratio of the "rise" divided by the "run" between two points on a line, or in other words, the ratio of the altitude change to the horizontal distance between any two points on the line.
   a. Slope0
   b. Thing
   c. Undefined
   d. Undefined

2. In mathematics, the concept of a _____ tries to capture the intuitive idea of a geometrical one-dimensional and continuous object. A simple example is the circle.
   a. Thing
   b. Curve0
   c. Undefined
   d. Undefined

3. In mathematics and the mathematical sciences, a _____ is a fixed, but possibly unspecified, value. This is in contrast to a variable, which is not fixed.
   a. Constant0
   b. Thing
   c. Undefined
   d. Undefined

4. The mathematical concept of a _____ expresses the intuitive idea of deterministic dependence between two quantities, one of which is viewed as primary and the other as secondary. A _____ then is a way to associate a unique output for each input of a specified type, for example, a real number or an element of a given set.
   a. Function0
   b. Thing
   c. Undefined
   d. Undefined

5. _____ are the basic objects of study in graph theory. Informally speaking, a graph is a set of objects called points, nodes, or vertices connected by links called lines or edges.
   a. Thing
   b. Graphs0
   c. Undefined
   d. Undefined

6. _____ has many meanings, most of which simply .
   a. Power0
   b. Thing
   c. Undefined
   d. Undefined

7. The _____ is a measurement of how a function changes when the values of its inputs change.
   a. Derivative0
   b. Thing
   c. Undefined
   d. Undefined

8. An _____ is a combination of numbers, operators, grouping symbols and/or free variables and bound variables arranged in a meaningful way which can be evaluated..
   a. Thing
   b. Expression0
   c. Undefined
   d. Undefined

9. In mathematics, a _____ is an expression that is constructed from one or more variables and constants, using only the operations of addition, subtraction, multiplication, and constant positive whole number exponents. is a _____. Note in particular that division by an expression containing a variable is not in general allowed in polynomials. [1]
   a. Thing
   b. Polynomial0
   c. Undefined
   d. Undefined

Chapter 3. SHORT-CUTS TO DIFFERENTIATION

10. _____, a field in mathematics, is the study of how functions change when their inputs change. The primary object of study in _____ is the derivative.
    a. Differential calculus0
    b. Thing
    c. Undefined
    d. Undefined

11. In mathematics, the _____ is a conic section generated by the intersection of a right circular conical surface and a plane parallel to a generating straight line of that surface. It can also be defined as locus of points in a plane which are equidistant from a given point.
    a. Thing
    b. Parabola0
    c. Undefined
    d. Undefined

12. _____ of an object is its speed in a particular direction.
    a. Thing
    b. Velocity0
    c. Undefined
    d. Undefined

13. _____ is defined as the rate of change or derivative with respect to time of velocity.
    a. Acceleration0
    b. Thing
    c. Undefined
    d. Undefined

14. In trigonometry, the _____ is a function defined as $\tan x = \sin x / \cos x$. The function is so-named because it can be defined as the length of a certain segment of a _____ (in the geometric sense) to the unit circle. In plane geometry, a line is _____ to a curve, at some point, if both line and curve pass through the point with the same direction.
    a. Tangent0
    b. Thing
    c. Undefined
    d. Undefined

15. An _____ is when two lines intersect somewhere on a plane creating a right angle at intersection
    a. Axes0
    b. Thing
    c. Undefined
    d. Undefined

16. _____ has two distinct but etymologically-related meanings: one in geometry and one in trigonometry.
    a. Thing
    b. Tangent line0
    c. Undefined
    d. Undefined

17. In mathematics, the _____ of a coordinate system is the point where the axes of the system intersect.
    a. Thing
    b. Origin0
    c. Undefined
    d. Undefined

18. In elementary algebra, an _____ is a set that contains every real number between two indicated numbers and may contain the two numbers themselves.
    a. Thing
    b. Interval0
    c. Undefined
    d. Undefined

19. The _____ of measurement are a globally standardized and modernized form of the metric system.
    a. Thing
    b. Units0
    c. Undefined
    d. Undefined

Chapter 3. SHORT-CUTS TO DIFFERENTIATION

20. The _____, the average in everyday English, which is also called the arithmetic _____ (and is distinguished from the geometric _____ or harmonic _____). The average is also called the sample _____. The expected value of a random variable, which is also called the population _____.
   a. Thing
   b. Mean0
   c. Undefined
   d. Undefined

21. The metre (or _____, see spelling differences) is a measure of length. It is the basic unit of length in the metric system and in the International System of Units (SI), used around the world for general and scientific purposes.
   a. Concept
   b. Meter0
   c. Undefined
   d. Undefined

22. A _____ is a unit of length, usually used to measure distance, in a number of different systems, including Imperial units, United States customary units and Norwegian/Swedish mil. Its size can vary from system to system, but in each is between 1 and 10 kilometers. In contemporary English contexts _____ refers to either:
   a. Thing
   b. Mile0
   c. Undefined
   d. Undefined

23. _____ is a unit of speed, expressing the number of international miles covered per hour.
   a. Miles per hour0
   b. Thing
   c. Undefined
   d. Undefined

24. In geometry, the _____ of an object is a point in some sense in the middle of the object.
   a. Center0
   b. Thing
   c. Undefined
   d. Undefined

25. _____ is the property of a physical object that quantifies the amount of matter and energy it is equivalent to.
   a. Mass0
   b. Thing
   c. Undefined
   d. Undefined

26. In Euclidean geometry, a _____ is the set of all points in a plane at a fixed distance, called the radius, from a given point, the center.
   a. Circle0
   b. Thing
   c. Undefined
   d. Undefined

27. In classical geometry, a _____ of a circle or sphere is any line segment from its center to its boundary. By extension, the _____ of a circle or sphere is the length of any such segment. The _____ is half the diameter. In science and engineering the term _____ of curvature is commonly used as a synonym for _____.
   a. Radius0
   b. Thing
   c. Undefined
   d. Undefined

28. In mathematics, _____ growth occurs when the growth rate of a function is always proportional to the function's current size.
   a. Exponential0
   b. Thing
   c. Undefined
   d. Undefined

Chapter 3. SHORT-CUTS TO DIFFERENTIATION 35

29. _____ is one of the most important functions in mathematics. A function commonly used to study growth and decay
   a. Exponential function0
   b. Thing
   c. Undefined
   d. Undefined

30. In mathematics, two quantities are called _____ if they vary in such a way that one of the quantities is a constant multiple of the other, or equivalently if they have a constant ratio.
   a. Thing
   b. Proportional0
   c. Undefined
   d. Undefined

31. In mathematics, an inequality is a statement about the relative size or order of two objects. For example 14 > 10, or 14 is _____ 10.
   a. Greater than0
   b. Thing
   c. Undefined
   d. Undefined

32. _____ is a special mathematical relationship between two quantities. Two quantities are called proportional if they vary in such a way that one of the quantities is a constant multiple of the other, or equivalently if they have a constant ratio.
   a. Proportionality0
   b. Thing
   c. Undefined
   d. Undefined

33. A _____ is a special kind of ratio, indicating a relationship between two measurements with different units, such as miles to gallons or cents to pounds.
   a. Rate0
   b. Thing
   c. Undefined
   d. Undefined

34. In mainstream economics, the word _____ refers to a general rise in prices measured against a standard level of purchasing power.
   a. Thing
   b. Inflation0
   c. Undefined
   d. Undefined

35. The population _____ is the total number of human beings alive on the planet Earth at a given time.
   a. Thing
   b. Of the world0
   c. Undefined
   d. Undefined

36. In sociology and biology a _____ is the collection of people or organisms of a particular species living in a given geographic area or space, usually measured by a census.
   a. Population0
   b. Thing
   c. Undefined
   d. Undefined

37. The _____ is the total number of human beings alive on the planet Earth at a given time.
   a. Population of the world0
   b. Thing
   c. Undefined
   d. Undefined

38. In mathematics, a _____ is the result of multiplying, or an expression that identifies factors to be multiplied.

Chapter 3. SHORT-CUTS TO DIFFERENTIATION

a. Product0
c. Undefined
b. Thing
d. Undefined

39. In geometry, two lines or planes if one falls on the other in such a way as to create congruent adjacent angles. The term may be used as a noun or adjective. Thus, referring to Figure 1, the line AB is the _____ to CD through the point B.
   a. Thing
   b. Perpendicular0
   c. Undefined
   d. Undefined

40. Mathematical _____ is used to represent ideas.
   a. Notation0
   b. Thing
   c. Undefined
   d. Undefined

41. In mathematics, a _____ is the end result of a division problem. It can also be expressed as the number of times the divisor divides into the dividend.
   a. Quotient0
   b. Thing
   c. Undefined
   d. Undefined

42. The function difference divided by the point difference is known as the _____
   a. Thing
   b. Difference quotient0
   c. Undefined
   d. Undefined

43. The _____ is a method of finding the derivative of a function that is the quotient of two other functions for which derivatives exist.
   a. Thing
   b. Quotient rule0
   c. Undefined
   d. Undefined

44. The _____ governs the differentiation of products of differentiable functions.
   a. Thing
   b. Product rule0
   c. Undefined
   d. Undefined

45. _____ is a business term for the amount of money that a company receives from its activities in a given period, mostly from sales of products and/or services to customers
   a. Thing
   b. Revenue0
   c. Undefined
   d. Undefined

46. _____ is the fee paid on borrowed money.
   a. Interest0
   b. Thing
   c. Undefined
   d. Undefined

47. In banking and accountancy, the outstanding _____ is the amount of money owned, or due, that remains in a deposit account or a loan account at a given date, after all past remittances, payments and withdrawal have been accounted for.
   a. Balance0
   b. Thing
   c. Undefined
   d. Undefined

48. In calculus, the _____ is a formula for the derivative of the composite of two functions.

Chapter 3. SHORT-CUTS TO DIFFERENTIATION 37

a. Concept
b. Chain rule0
c. Undefined
d. Undefined

49. In mathematics, a _____ of a positive integer n is a way of writing n as a sum of positive integers.
a. Composition0
b. Thing
c. Undefined
d. Undefined

50. Equivalence is the condition of being _____ or essentially equal.
a. Thing
b. Equivalent0
c. Undefined
d. Undefined

51. A _____ is the part of a fraction that tells how many equal parts make up a whole, and which is used in the name of the fraction: "halves", "thirds", "fourths" or "quarters", "fifths" and so on.
a. Concept
b. Denominator0
c. Undefined
d. Undefined

52. _____ of a random variable or somewhat more precisely, of a probability distribution is a measure of its statistical dispersion, indicating how its possible values are spread around the expected value.
a. Variance0
b. Thing
c. Undefined
d. Undefined

53. The _____, also called Gaussian distribution by scientists, is a continuous probability distribution of great importance in many fields.
a. Thing
b. Normal distribution0
c. Undefined
d. Undefined

54. _____ is a mathematical science pertaining to the collection, analysis, interpretation or explanation, and presentation of data. It is applicable to a wide variety of academic disciplines, from the physical and social sciences to the humanities.
a. Thing
b. Statistics0
c. Undefined
d. Undefined

55. In mathematical analysis, _____ are objects which generalize functions and probability distributions.
a. Thing
b. Distribution0
c. Undefined
d. Undefined

56. An _____ is the fee paid on borrow money.
a. Concept
b. Interest rate0
c. Undefined
d. Undefined

57. The _____ in a vacuum is an important physical constant denoted by the letter c for constant or the Latin word celeritas meaning "swiftness
a. Speed of light0
b. Thing
c. Undefined
d. Undefined

Chapter 3. SHORT-CUTS TO DIFFERENTIATION

58. _____ is electromagnetic radiation with a wavelength that is visible to the eye (visible _____) or, in a technical or scientific context, electromagnetic radiation of any wavelength.
   a. Light0
   b. Thing
   c. Undefined
   d. Undefined

59. A _____ is a set of numbers that designate location in a given reference system, such as x,y in a planar _____ system or an x,y,z in a three-dimensional _____ system.
   a. Thing
   b. Coordinate0
   c. Undefined
   d. Undefined

60. The _____ of a member of a multiset is how many memberships in the multiset it has.
   a. Thing
   b. Multiplicity0
   c. Undefined
   d. Undefined

61. The _____ of an angle is the ratio of the length of the adjacent side to the length of the hypotenuse.
   a. Concept
   b. Cosine0
   c. Undefined
   d. Undefined

62. In mathematics, there are several meanings of _____ depending on the subject.
   a. Degree0
   b. Thing
   c. Undefined
   d. Undefined

63. _____ is a trigonemtric function that is important when studying triangles and modeling periodic phenomena, among other applications.
   a. Thing
   b. Sine0
   c. Undefined
   d. Undefined

64. In mathematics, a _____ is a mathematical statement which appears likely to be true, but has not been formally proven to be true under the rules of mathematical logic.
   a. Conjecture0
   b. Concept
   c. Undefined
   d. Undefined

65. _____ are a measure of time.
   a. Minutes0
   b. Thing
   c. Undefined
   d. Undefined

66. _____ is the difference of electrical potential between two points of an electrical or electronic circuit, expressed in volts
   a. Thing
   b. Voltage0
   c. Undefined
   d. Undefined

67. A _____ is a function that assigns a number to subsets of a given set.
   a. Measure0
   b. Thing
   c. Undefined
   d. Undefined

Chapter 3. SHORT-CUTS TO DIFFERENTIATION

68. In economics, economic _____ is simply a state of the world where economic forces are balanced and in the absence of external influences the values of economic variables will not change.
    a. Equilibrium0
    b. Thing
    c. Undefined
    d. Undefined

69. _____ element of an element x with respect to a binary operation * with identity element e is an element y such that x * y = y * x = e. In particular,
    a. Thing
    b. Inverse0
    c. Undefined
    d. Undefined

70. An _____ is a function which does the reverse of a given function.
    a. Thing
    b. Inverse function0
    c. Undefined
    d. Undefined

71. A _____ is a deliberate process for transforming one or more inputs into one or more results.
    a. Thing
    b. Calculation0
    c. Undefined
    d. Undefined

72. An _____ is an equality that remains true regardless of the values of any variables that appear within it, to distinguish it from an equality which is true under more particular conditions.
    a. Identity0
    b. Thing
    c. Undefined
    d. Undefined

73. In mathematics, the _____ functions are functions of an angle; they are important when studying triangles and modeling periodic phenomena, among many other applications.
    a. Thing
    b. Trigonometric0
    c. Undefined
    d. Undefined

74. The _____ are functions of an angle; they are important when studying triangles and modeling periodic phenomena, among many other applications.
    a. Thing
    b. Trigonometric functions0
    c. Undefined
    d. Undefined

75. In mathematics, the _____ are the inverse functions of the trigonometric functions.
    a. Inverse trigonometric functions0
    b. Thing
    c. Undefined
    d. Undefined

76. In mathematics, science including computer science, linguistics and engineering, an _____ is, generally speaking, an independent variable or input to a function.
    a. Argument0
    b. Thing
    c. Undefined
    d. Undefined

77. In mathematics, the multiplicative inverse of a number x, denoted 1/x or x^{-1}, is the number which, when multiplied by x, yields 1. The multiplicative inverse of x is also called the _____ of x.

Chapter 3. SHORT-CUTS TO DIFFERENTIATION

a. Reciprocal0
b. Thing
c. Undefined
d. Undefined

78. In mathematics, an _____ is a generalization for the concept of a function in which the dependent variable may not be given explicitly in terms of the independent variable.
a. Thing
b. Implicit function0
c. Undefined
d. Undefined

79. _____ is to give an equation R(x,y) = S(x,y) that at least in part has the same graph as y = f(x).
a. Implicit differentiation0
b. Thing
c. Undefined
d. Undefined

80. A quadratic equation with real solutions, called roots, which may be real or complex, is given by the _____ : $x = \frac{-b \pm \sqrt{b^2 - 4ac}}{2a}$.
a. Quadratic formula0
b. Thing
c. Undefined
d. Undefined

81. In astronomy, geography, geometry and related sciences and contexts, a plane is said to be _____ at a given point if it is locally perpendicular to the gradient of the gravity field, i.e., with the direction of the gravitational force at that point.
a. Thing
b. Horizontal0
c. Undefined
d. Undefined

82. A _____ is an analog of an ordinary trigonometric, or circular, function.
a. Thing
b. Hyperbolic function0
c. Undefined
d. Undefined

83. In mathematics, a _____ number is a number which can be expressed as a ratio of two integers. Non-integer _____ numbers (commonly called fractions) are usually written as the vulgar fraction a / b, where b is not zero.
a. Rational0
b. Thing
c. Undefined
d. Undefined

84. _____ is a method for differentiating expressions involving exponentiation the power operation.
a. Power rule0
b. Thing
c. Undefined
d. Undefined

85. _____ is the design, analysis, and/or construction of works for practical purposes.
a. Engineering0
b. Thing
c. Undefined
d. Undefined

86. In combinatorial mathematics, a _____ is an un-ordered collection of unique elements.
a. Combination0
b. Concept
c. Undefined
d. Undefined

87. _____ is the shape of a hanging flexible chain or cable when supported at its ends and acted upon by a uniform gravitational force. The chain is steepest near the points of suspension because this part of the chain has the most weight pulling down on it. Toward the bottom, the slope of the chain decreases because the chain is supporting less weight.

Chapter 3. SHORT-CUTS TO DIFFERENTIATION

    a. Catenary0
    b. Thing
    c. Undefined
    d. Undefined

88. _____ are functions which satisfy particular symmetry relations, with respect to taking additive inverses.
    a. Even function0
    b. Thing
    c. Undefined
    d. Undefined

89. _____ is bother the congnitive process of transferring information from a particular subject , and a linguistic expression corresponding to such a process.
    a. Analogy0
    b. Thing
    c. Undefined
    d. Undefined

90. A _____ is a type of bridge that has been created since ancient times as early as 100 AD.
    a. Suspension bridge0
    b. Thing
    c. Undefined
    d. Undefined

91. _____ is a reaction force applied by a stretched string on the objects which stretch it.
    a. Thing
    b. Tension0
    c. Undefined
    d. Undefined

92. The word _____ comes from the Latin word linearis, which means created by lines.
    a. Linear0
    b. Thing
    c. Undefined
    d. Undefined

93. _____ is an approximation of a general function using a linear function more precisely, an affine function.
    a. Thing
    b. Linear approximation0
    c. Undefined
    d. Undefined

94. A _____ is a negotiable instrument instructing a financial institution to pay a specific amount of a specific currency from a specific demand account held in the maker/depositor's name with that institution. Both the maker and payee may be natural persons or legal entities.
    a. Thing
    b. Check0
    c. Undefined
    d. Undefined

95. In mathematics, a _____ is a statement that can be proved on the basis of explicitly stated or previously agreed assumptions.
    a. Theorem0
    b. Thing
    c. Undefined
    d. Undefined

96. In mathematics and its applications, _____ refers to finding the linear approximation to a function at a given point.
    a. Thing
    b. Linearization0
    c. Undefined
    d. Undefined

97. The _____ of a mathematical object is its size: a property by which it can be larger or smaller than other objects of the same kind; in technical terms, an ordering of the class of objects to which it belongs.

Chapter 3. SHORT-CUTS TO DIFFERENTIATION

    a. Magnitude0   b. Thing
    c. Undefined   d. Undefined

98. _____ algebra (sometimes called General algebra) is the field of mathematics that studies the ideas common to all algebraic structures.
    a. Thing   b. Universal0
    c. Undefined   d. Undefined

99. _____ is a way of expressing a number as a fraction of 100 per cent meaning "per hundred".
    a. Thing   b. Percent0
    c. Undefined   d. Undefined

100. In the mathematical field of numerical analysis, the _____ in some data is the discrepancy between an exact value and some approximation to it.
    a. Approximation Error0   b. Thing
    c. Undefined   d. Undefined

101. _____ is a function whose values do not vary and thus are constant.
    a. Thing   b. Constant function0
    c. Undefined   d. Undefined

102. A _____ signifies a point or points of probability on a subject e.g., the _____ of creativity, which allows for the formation of rule or norm or law by interpretation of the phenomena events that can be created.
    a. Thing   b. Principle0
    c. Undefined   d. Undefined

103. In mathematics, an _____ is a statement about the relative size or order of two objects.
    a. Thing   b. Inequality0
    c. Undefined   d. Undefined

104. _____ is a mathematical subject that includes the study of limits, derivatives, integrals, and power series and constitutes a major part of modern university curriculum.
    a. Calculus0   b. Thing
    c. Undefined   d. Undefined

105. In common philosophical language, a proposition or _____, is the content of an assertion, that is, it is true-or-false and defined by the meaning of a particular piece of language.
    a. Statement0   b. Concept
    c. Undefined   d. Undefined

106. A _____ function is a function for which, intuitively, small changes in the input result in small changes in the output.
    a. Event   b. Continuous0
    c. Undefined   d. Undefined

Chapter 3. SHORT-CUTS TO DIFFERENTIATION

107. In mathematics, an _____, mean, or central tendency of a data set refers to a measure of the "middle" or "expected" value of the data set.
 a. Concept
 b. Average0
 c. Undefined
 d. Undefined

108. _____ comes from the Latin word linearis, which means created by lines.
 a. Thing
 b. Linearity0
 c. Undefined
 d. Undefined

109. In mathematics, _____ are the intuitive idea of a geometrical one-dimensional and continuous object.
 a. Curves0
 b. Thing
 c. Undefined
 d. Undefined

110. In mathematics, the _____ of two sets A and B is the set that contains all elements of A that also belong to B (or equivalently, all elements of B that also belong to A), but no other elements.
 a. Thing
 b. Intersection0
 c. Undefined
 d. Undefined

111. The _____ or kilogramme is the SI base unit of mass. It is defined as being equal to the mass of the international prototype of the _____.
 a. Thing
 b. Kilogram0
 c. Undefined
 d. Undefined

112. A _____ is a unit of length in the metric system, equal to one thousand metres, the current SI base unit of length
 a. Kilometer0
 b. Thing
 c. Undefined
 d. Undefined

113. A _____ is traditionally an infinitesimally small change in a variable.
 a. Differential0
 b. Thing
 c. Undefined
 d. Undefined

114. A _____ is a mathematical equation for an unknown function of one or several variables which relates the values of the function itself and of its derivatives of various orders.
 a. Differential equation0
 b. Thing
 c. Undefined
 d. Undefined

115. In geometry, an _____ of a triangle is a straight line through a vertex and perpendicular to (i.e. forming a right angle with) the opposite side or an extension of the opposite side.
 a. Altitude0
 b. Concept
 c. Undefined
 d. Undefined

116. _____ is a physical property of a system that underlies the common notions of hot and cold; something that is hotter has the greater _____.
 a. Thing
 b. Temperature0
 c. Undefined
 d. Undefined

Chapter 3. SHORT-CUTS TO DIFFERENTIATION

117. U.S. liquid _____ is legally defined as 231 cubic inches, and is equal to 3.785411784 litres or abotu 0.13368 cubic feet. This is the most common definition of a _____. The U.S. fluid ounce is defined as 1/128 of a U.S. _____.
   a. Thing
   b. Gallon0
   c. Undefined
   d. Undefined

118. In mathematics, the _____ inverse, or opposite, of a number n is the number that, when added to n, yields zero. The _____ inverse of n is denoted −n.
   a. Additive0
   b. Thing
   c. Undefined
   d. Undefined

119. _____ is a branch of mathematics concerning the study of structure, relation and quantity.
   a. Concept
   b. Algebra0
   c. Undefined
   d. Undefined

120. In logic, and especially in its applications to mathematics and philosophy, a _____ is an exception to a proposed general rule, i.e., a specific instance of the falsity of a universal quantification (a "for all" statement).
   a. Thing
   b. Counterexample0
   c. Undefined
   d. Undefined

121. A _____ is a first degree polynomial mathematical function of the form: f(x) = mx + b where m and b are real constants and x is a real variable.
   a. Linear function0
   b. Thing
   c. Undefined
   d. Undefined

122. A _____ is a function for which, intuitively, small changes in the input result in small changes in the output.
   a. Event
   b. Continuous function0
   c. Undefined
   d. Undefined

123. In a mathematical proof or a syllogism, a _____ is a statement that is the logical consequence of preceding statements.
   a. Concept
   b. Conclusion0
   c. Undefined
   d. Undefined

124. _____ is a kind of property which exists as magnitude or multitude. It is among the basic classes of things along with quality, substance, change, and relation.
   a. Amount0
   b. Thing
   c. Undefined
   d. Undefined

125. Sir Isaac _____, was an English physicist, mathematician, astronomer, natural philosopher, and alchemist, regarded by many as the greatest figure in the history of science
   a. Newton0
   b. Person
   c. Undefined
   d. Undefined

126. Initial objects are also called _____, and terminal objects are also called final.

a. Coterminal0
c. Undefined
b. Thing
d. Undefined

Chapter 4. USING THE DERIVATIVE

1. In elementary algebra, an _____ is a set that contains every real number between two indicated numbers and may contain the two numbers themselves.
   a. Thing
   b. Interval0
   c. Undefined
   d. Undefined

2. In geographic information systems, a _____ comprises an entity with a geographic location, typically determined by points, arcs, or polygons. Carriageways and cadastres exemplify _____ data.
   a. Feature0
   b. Thing
   c. Undefined
   d. Undefined

3. The mathematical concept of a _____ expresses the intuitive idea of deterministic dependence between two quantities, one of which is viewed as primary and the other as secondary. A _____ then is a way to associate a unique output for each input of a specified type, for example, a real number or an element of a given set.
   a. Thing
   b. Function0
   c. Undefined
   d. Undefined

4. The _____ is a measurement of how a function changes when the values of its inputs change.
   a. Derivative0
   b. Thing
   c. Undefined
   d. Undefined

5. In mathematics, a _____ is an expression that is constructed from one or more variables and constants, using only the operations of addition, subtraction, multiplication, and constant positive whole number exponents. is a _____. Note in particular that division by an expression containing a variable is not in general allowed in polynomials. [1]
   a. Thing
   b. Polynomial0
   c. Undefined
   d. Undefined

6. A _____ function is a function for which, intuitively, small changes in the input result in small changes in the output.
   a. Event
   b. Continuous0
   c. Undefined
   d. Undefined

7. In mathematics, _____ is the decomposition of an object into a product of other objects, or factors, which when multiplied together give the original.
   a. Thing
   b. Factoring0
   c. Undefined
   d. Undefined

8. Any point where a graph makes contact with an coordinate axis is called an _____ of the graph
   a. Intercept0
   b. Thing
   c. Undefined
   d. Undefined

9. _____ is a point on the domain of a function
   a. Thing
   b. Critical point0
   c. Undefined
   d. Undefined

10. In mathematics, a _____ of a k-place relation $L \subseteq X_1 \times \ldots \times X_k$ is one of the sets X_j, $1 \leq j \leq k$. In the special case where k = 2 and $L \subseteq X_1 \times X_2$ is a function $L : X_1 \rightarrow X_2$, it is conventional to refer to X_1 as the _____ of the function and to refer to X_2 as the codomain of the function.

Chapter 4. USING THE DERIVATIVE

a. Thing
c. Undefined
b. Domain0
d. Undefined

11. In trigonometry, the _____ is a function defined as tan x = $^{\sin x}/_{\cos x}$. The function is so-named because it can be defined as the length of a certain segment of a _____ (in the geometric sense) to the unit circle. In plane geometry, a line is _____ to a curve, at some point, if both line and curve pass through the point with the same direction.

a. Thing
c. Undefined
b. Tangent0
d. Undefined

12. In astronomy, geography, geometry and related sciences and contexts, a plane is said to be _____ at a given point if it is locally perpendicular to the gradient of the gravity field, i.e., with the direction of the gravitational force at that point.

a. Thing
c. Undefined
b. Horizontal0
d. Undefined

13. In mathematics, defined and _____ are used to explain whether or not expressions have meaningful, sensible, and unambiguous values.

a. Thing
c. Undefined
b. Undefined0
d. Undefined

14. In mathematics, the _____ (or modulus) of a real number is its numerical value without regard to its sign.

a. Thing
c. Undefined
b. Absolute value0
d. Undefined

15. A real-valued function f defined on the real line is said to have a _____ point at the point x∗, if there exists some ε > 0, such that f when x − x∗ < ε.

a. Local maximum0
c. Undefined
b. Thing
d. Undefined

16. _____ is a free computer algebra system based on a 1982 version of Macsyma

a. Maxima0
c. Undefined
b. Thing
d. Undefined

17. _____ are points in the domain of a function at which the function takes a largest value or smallest value, either within a given neighborhood or on the function domain in its entirety.

a. Thing
c. Undefined
b. Maxima and minima0
d. Undefined

18. In mathematics, maxima and _____, known collectively as extrema, are points in the domain of a function at which the function takes a largest value .

a. Thing
c. Undefined
b. Minima0
d. Undefined

19. The _____, the average in everyday English, which is also called the arithmetic _____ (and is distinguished from the geometric _____ or harmonic _____). The average is also called the sample _____. The expected value of a random variable, which is also called the population _____.

48 **Chapter 4. USING THE DERIVATIVE**

    a. Mean0
    c. Undefined
    b. Thing
    d. Undefined

20. Acid _____ ratio measures the ability of a company to use its near cash or quick assets to immediately extinguish its current liabilities.
    a. Thing
    c. Undefined
    b. Test0
    d. Undefined

21. _____ determines whether a given critical point of a function is a maximum, a minimum, or neither.
    a. First Derivative Test0
    c. Undefined
    b. Thing
    d. Undefined

22. The word _____ means curving in or hollowed inward.
    a. Concavity0
    c. Undefined
    b. Thing
    d. Undefined

23. _____ is often used to describe the measurement of the steepness, incline, gradient, or grade of a straight line. The _____ is defined as the ratio of the "rise" divided by the "run" between two points on a line, or in other words, the ratio of the altitude change to the horizontal distance between any two points on the line.
    a. Slope0
    c. Undefined
    b. Thing
    d. Undefined

24. _____ is a a point on a curve at which the tangent crosses the curve itself.
    a. Thing
    c. Undefined
    b. Inflection point0
    d. Undefined

25. In mathematics, the _____ f is the collection of all ordered pairs . In particular, graph means the graphical representation of this collection, in the form of a curve or surface, together with axes, etc. Graphing on a Cartesian plane is sometimes referred to as curve sketching.
    a. Graph of a function0
    c. Undefined
    b. Thing
    d. Undefined

26. In mathematics, _____ expressions is used to reduce the expression into the lowest possible term.
    a. Thing
    c. Undefined
    b. Simplifying0
    d. Undefined

27. In mathematics, the concept of a _____ tries to capture the intuitive idea of a geometrical one-dimensional and continuous object. A simple example is the circle.
    a. Thing
    c. Undefined
    b. Curve0
    d. Undefined

28. _____ has two distinct but etymologically-related meanings: one in geometry and one in trigonometry.
    a. Tangent line0
    c. Undefined
    b. Thing
    d. Undefined

Chapter 4. USING THE DERIVATIVE

29. The _____ of a solid object is the three-dimensional concept of how much space it occupies, often quantified numerically.
   a. Thing
   b. Volume0
   c. Undefined
   d. Undefined

30. A _____ is a special kind of ratio, indicating a relationship between two measurements with different units, such as miles to gallons or cents to pounds.
   a. Rate0
   b. Thing
   c. Undefined
   d. Undefined

31. In mathematics and the mathematical sciences, a _____ is a fixed, but possibly unspecified, value. This is in contrast to a variable, which is not fixed.
   a. Constant0
   b. Thing
   c. Undefined
   d. Undefined

32. In geometry, a _____ (Greek words diairo = divide and metro = measure) of a circle is any straight line segment that passes through the centre and whose endpoints are on the circular boundary, or, in more modern usage, the length of such a line segment. When using the word in the more modern sense, one speaks of the _____ rather than a _____, because all diameters of a circle have the same length. This length is twice the radius. The _____ of a circle is also the longest chord that the circle has.
   a. Thing
   b. Diameter0
   c. Undefined
   d. Undefined

33. _____ are the basic objects of study in graph theory. Informally speaking, a graph is a set of objects called points, nodes, or vertices connected by links called lines or edges.
   a. Graphs0
   b. Thing
   c. Undefined
   d. Undefined

34. In mathematics, the _____ is a conic section generated by the intersection of a right circular conical surface and a plane parallel to a generating straight line of that surface. It can also be defined as locus of points in a plane which are equidistant from a given point.
   a. Thing
   b. Parabola0
   c. Undefined
   d. Undefined

35. In sociology and biology a _____ is the collection of people or organisms of a particular species living in a given geographic area or space, usually measured by a census.
   a. Population0
   b. Thing
   c. Undefined
   d. Undefined

36. A _____ is a three-dimensional geometric shape formed by straight lines through a fixed point (vertex) to the points of a fixed curve (directrix)
   a. Cone0
   b. Concept
   c. Undefined
   d. Undefined

37. In mathematics, _____ are the intuitive idea of a geometrical one-dimensional and continuous object.

Chapter 4. USING THE DERIVATIVE

    a. Thing
    b. Curves0
    c. Undefined
    d. Undefined

38. A _____ is the quantity that defines certain relatively constant characteristics of systems or functions..
    a. Thing
    b. Parameter0
    c. Undefined
    d. Undefined

39. _____ is a synonym for information.
    a. Thing
    b. Data0
    c. Undefined
    d. Undefined

40. The metre (or _____, see spelling differences) is a measure of length. It is the basic unit of length in the metric system and in the International System of Units (SI), used around the world for general and scientific purposes.
    a. Meter0
    b. Concept
    c. Undefined
    d. Undefined

41. _____ is the chance that something is likely to happen or be the case.
    a. Thing
    b. Probability0
    c. Undefined
    d. Undefined

42. _____ is a mathematical science pertaining to the collection, analysis, interpretation or explanation, and presentation of data. It is applicable to a wide variety of academic disciplines, from the physical and social sciences to the humanities.
    a. Thing
    b. Statistics0
    c. Undefined
    d. Undefined

43. _____ is mass m per unit volume V.
    a. Thing
    b. Density0
    c. Undefined
    d. Undefined

44. An _____ is a straight line or curve A to which another curve B approaches closer and closer as one moves along it. As one moves along B, the space between it and the _____ A becomes smaller and smaller, and can in fact be made as small as one could wish by going far enough along. A curve may or may not touch or cross its _____. In fact, the curve may intersect the _____ an infinite number of times.
    a. Asymptote0
    b. Thing
    c. Undefined
    d. Undefined

45. The _____ of measurement are a globally standardized and modernized form of the metric system.
    a. Thing
    b. Units0
    c. Undefined
    d. Undefined

46. In geometry, the _____ of an object is a point in some sense in the middle of the object.
    a. Thing
    b. Center0
    c. Undefined
    d. Undefined

Chapter 4. USING THE DERIVATIVE

47. _____ is a physical property of a system that underlies the common notions of hot and cold; something that is hotter has the greater _____.
   a. Temperature0
   b. Thing
   c. Undefined
   d. Undefined

48. _____ of an object is its speed in a particular direction.
   a. Velocity0
   b. Thing
   c. Undefined
   d. Undefined

49. An _____ is when two lines intersect somewhere on a plane creating a right angle at intersection
   a. Thing
   b. Axes0
   c. Undefined
   d. Undefined

50. _____ is the property of a physical object that quantifies the amount of matter and energy it is equivalent to.
   a. Thing
   b. Mass0
   c. Undefined
   d. Undefined

51. In mathematics and elsewhere, the adjective _____ means fourth order, such as the function x4. A _____ number is a number which equals the fourth power of an integer.
   a. Quartic0
   b. Thing
   c. Undefined
   d. Undefined

52. In mathematics, a _____ is a constant multiplicative factor of a certain object. The object can be such things as a variable, a vector, a function, etc. For example, the _____ of $9x^2$ is 9.
   a. Thing
   b. Coefficient0
   c. Undefined
   d. Undefined

53. _____ are a measure of time.
   a. Thing
   b. Minutes0
   c. Undefined
   d. Undefined

54. A _____ is a set of numbers that designate location in a given reference system, such as x,y in a planar _____ system or an x,y,z in a three-dimensional _____ system.
   a. Thing
   b. Coordinate0
   c. Undefined
   d. Undefined

55. In mathematics, a set is called _____ if there is a bijection between the set and some set of the form {1, 2, ..., n} where n is a natural number.
   a. Thing
   b. Finite0
   c. Undefined
   d. Undefined

56. In physics, a _____ may refer to the scalar _____ or to the vector _____.
   a. Thing
   b. Potential0
   c. Undefined
   d. Undefined

Chapter 4. USING THE DERIVATIVE

57. An _____ is a combination of numbers, operators, grouping symbols and/or free variables and bound variables arranged in a meaningful way which can be evaluated..
    a. Thing
    b. Expression0
    c. Undefined
    d. Undefined

58. In physics, _____ is an influence that may cause an object to accelerate. It may be experienced as a lift, a push, or a pull. The actual acceleration of the body is determined by the vector sum of all forces acting on it, known as net _____ or resultant _____.
    a. Thing
    b. Force0
    c. Undefined
    d. Undefined

59. In computer science, an _____ is the problem of finding the best solution from all feasible solutions.
    a. Thing
    b. Optimization problem0
    c. Undefined
    d. Undefined

60. In mathematics, an inequality is a statement about the relative size or order of two objects. For example 14 > 10, or 14 is _____ 10.
    a. Thing
    b. Greater than0
    c. Undefined
    d. Undefined

61. A _____ is a function for which, intuitively, small changes in the input result in small changes in the output.
    a. Event
    b. Continuous function0
    c. Undefined
    d. Undefined

62. In geometry, an _____ is a point at which a line segment or ray terminates.
    a. Thing
    b. Endpoint0
    c. Undefined
    d. Undefined

63. In mathematics, a _____ may be described informally as a number that can be given by an infinite decimal representation.
    a. Thing
    b. Real number0
    c. Undefined
    d. Undefined

64. In mathematics, the _____ of a function is the set of all "output" values produced by that function. Given a function $f : A \to B$, the _____ of f, is defined to be the set $\{x \in B : x = f(a) \text{ for some } a \in A\}$.
    a. Thing
    b. Range0
    c. Undefined
    d. Undefined

65. _____ is a mathematical subject that includes the study of limits, derivatives, integrals, and power series and constitutes a major part of modern university curriculum.
    a. Calculus0
    b. Thing
    c. Undefined
    d. Undefined

66. In mathematics, an _____, mean, or central tendency of a data set refers to a measure of the "middle" or "expected" value of the data set.

Chapter 4. USING THE DERIVATIVE

a. Average0
b. Concept
c. Undefined
d. Undefined

67. A _____ is a unit of length, usually used to measure distance, in a number of different systems, including Imperial units, United States customary units and Norwegian/Swedish mil. Its size can vary from system to system, but in each is between 1 and 10 kilometers. In contemporary English contexts _____ refers to either:
a. Thing
b. Mile0
c. Undefined
d. Undefined

68. In mathematics, especially in order theory, an _____ of a subset S of some partially ordered set is an element of P which is greater than or equal to every element of S.
a. Thing
b. Upper bound0
c. Undefined
d. Undefined

69. The term _____ is defined dually as an element of P which is lesser than or equal to every element of S.
a. Lower bound0
b. Thing
c. Undefined
d. Undefined

70. In economics, economic _____ is simply a state of the world where economic forces are balanced and in the absence of external influences the values of economic variables will not change.
a. Thing
b. Equilibrium0
c. Undefined
d. Undefined

71. In mathematics, a _____ is the result of multiplying, or an expression that identifies factors to be multiplied.
a. Product0
b. Thing
c. Undefined
d. Undefined

72. The _____ governs the differentiation of products of differentiable functions.
a. Product rule0
b. Thing
c. Undefined
d. Undefined

73. In mathematics, an _____ is a statement about the relative size or order of two objects.
a. Thing
b. Inequality0
c. Undefined
d. Undefined

74. The _____ of a mathematical object is its size: a property by which it can be larger or smaller than other objects of the same kind; in technical terms, an ordering of the class of objects to which it belongs.
a. Magnitude0
b. Thing
c. Undefined
d. Undefined

75. _____ is the process of reducing the number of significant digits in a number.
a. Concept
b. Rounding0
c. Undefined
d. Undefined

76. A _____ is the part of a fraction that tells how many equal parts make up a whole, and which is used in the name of the fraction: "halves", "thirds", "fourths" or "quarters", "fifths" and so on.

Chapter 4. USING THE DERIVATIVE

a. Concept
c. Undefined
b. Denominator0
d. Undefined

77. In mathematics, a _____ is a demonstration that, assuming certain axioms, some statement is necessarily true.
a. Thing
c. Undefined
b. Proof0
d. Undefined

78. Initial objects are also called _____, and terminal objects are also called final.
a. Coterminal0
c. Undefined
b. Thing
d. Undefined

79. In classical geometry, a _____ of a circle or sphere is any line segment from its center to its boundary. By extension, the _____ of a circle or sphere is the length of any such segment. The _____ is half the diameter. In science and engineering the term _____ of curvature is commonly used as a synonym for _____.
a. Thing
c. Undefined
b. Radius0
d. Undefined

80. Order theory is a branch of mathematics that studies various kinds of binary relations that capture the intuitive notion of a mathematical _____.
a. Ordering0
c. Undefined
b. Thing
d. Undefined

81. The _____ of a ring R is defined to be the smallest positive integer n such that $n\,a = 0$, for all a in R.
a. Thing
c. Undefined
b. Characteristic0
d. Undefined

82. In mathematics, the _____ of a coordinate system is the point where the axes of the system intersect.
a. Origin0
c. Undefined
b. Thing
d. Undefined

83. In mathematics, the additive inverse, or _____ of a number n is the number that, when added to n, yields zero. The additive inverse of n is denoted −n. For example, 7 is −7, because 7 + (−7) = 0, and the additive inverse of −0.3 is 0.3, because −0.3 + 0.3 = 0.
a. Thing
c. Undefined
b. Opposite0
d. Undefined

84. In mathematics, the _____ of a number n is the number that, when added to n, yields zero. The _____ of n is denoted −n. For example, 7 is −7, because 7 + (−7) = 0, and the _____ of −0.3 is 0.3, because −0.3 + 0.3 = 0.
a. Additive inverse0
c. Undefined
b. Thing
d. Undefined

85. _____ is the SI unit of energy.
a. Thing
c. Undefined
b. Joule0
d. Undefined

Chapter 4. USING THE DERIVATIVE

86. _____ is a kind of property which exists as magnitude or multitude. It is among the basic classes of things along with quality, substance, change, and relation.
   a. Thing
   b. Amount0
   c. Undefined
   d. Undefined

87. _____ is the force that opposes the relative motion or tendency toward such motion of two surfaces in contact.
   a. Thing
   b. Friction0
   c. Undefined
   d. Undefined

88. In mathematics, two quantities are called _____ if they vary in such a way that one of the quantities is a constant multiple of the other, or equivalently if they have a constant ratio.
   a. Thing
   b. Proportional0
   c. Undefined
   d. Undefined

89. In plane geometry, a _____ is a polygon with four equal sides, four right angles, and parallel opposite sides. In algebra, the _____ of a number is that number multiplied by itself.
   a. Square0
   b. Thing
   c. Undefined
   d. Undefined

90. A _____ is the result of the addition of a set of numbers. The numbers may be natural numbers, complex numbers, matrices, or still more complicated objects. An infinite _____ is a subtle procedure known as a series.
   a. Thing
   b. Sum0
   c. Undefined
   d. Undefined

91. _____ is the speed of an aircraft relative to the air.
   a. Airspeed0
   b. Thing
   c. Undefined
   d. Undefined

92. _____, or Fuel efficiency can sometimes mean the same as thermal efficiency, that is, the efficiency of converting energy contained in a carrier fuel to kinetic energy or work.
   a. Thing
   b. Fuel consumption0
   c. Undefined
   d. Undefined

93. U.S. liquid _____ is legally defined as 231 cubic inches, and is equal to 3.785411784 litres or abotu 0.13368 cubic feet. This is the most common definition of a _____. The U.S. fluid ounce is defined as 1/128 of a U.S. _____.
   a. Thing
   b. Gallon0
   c. Undefined
   d. Undefined

94. _____ is a unit of speed, expressing the number of international miles covered per hour.
   a. Miles per hour0
   b. Thing
   c. Undefined
   d. Undefined

95. In common philosophical language, a proposition or _____, is the content of an assertion, that is, it is true-or-false and defined by the meaning of a particular piece of language.

Chapter 4. USING THE DERIVATIVE

    a. Statement0　　　　　　　　　　　　　　b. Concept
    c. Undefined　　　　　　　　　　　　　　　d. Undefined

96. The term _____ refers to the largest and the smallest element of a set.
    a. Thing　　　　　　　　　　　　　　　　　b. Extreme value0
    c. Undefined　　　　　　　　　　　　　　　d. Undefined

97. In mathematical analysis and related areas of mathematics, a set is called _____, if it is, in a certain sense, of finite size.
    a. Bounded0　　　　　　　　　　　　　　　b. Thing
    c. Undefined　　　　　　　　　　　　　　　d. Undefined

98. In mathematics, a _____ is a statement that can be proved on the basis of explicitly stated or previously agreed assumptions.
    a. Theorem0　　　　　　　　　　　　　　　b. Thing
    c. Undefined　　　　　　　　　　　　　　　d. Undefined

99. _____, from Latin meaning "to make progress", is defined in two different ways. Pure economic _____ is the increase in wealth that an investor has from making an investment, taking into consideration all costs associated with that investment including the opportunity cost of capital.
    a. Thing　　　　　　　　　　　　　　　　　b. Profit0
    c. Undefined　　　　　　　　　　　　　　　d. Undefined

100. _____ is a business term for the amount of money that a company receives from its activities in a given period, mostly from sales of products and/or services to customers
    a. Revenue0　　　　　　　　　　　　　　　b. Thing
    c. Undefined　　　　　　　　　　　　　　　d. Undefined

101. In Euclidean geometry, a uniform _____ is a linear transformation that enlargers or diminishes objects, and whose _____ factor is the same in all directions. This is also called homothethy.
    a. Thing　　　　　　　　　　　　　　　　　b. Scale0
    c. Undefined　　　　　　　　　　　　　　　d. Undefined

102. In finance, a _____ is collateral that the holder of a position in securities, options, or futures contracts has to deposit to cover the credit risk of his counterparty.
    a. Margin0　　　　　　　　　　　　　　　　b. Thing
    c. Undefined　　　　　　　　　　　　　　　d. Undefined

103. _____ is the use of marginal concepts within economics. Marginal concepts include marginal cost, marginal productivity and marginal utility, the law of diminishing rates of substitution, and the law of diminishing marginal utility.
    a. Marginal analysis0　　　　　　　　　　　b. Thing
    c. Undefined　　　　　　　　　　　　　　　d. Undefined

104. _____ is the change in total cost that arises when the quantity produced changes by one unit.

Chapter 4. USING THE DERIVATIVE

a. Thing
b. Marginal cost0
c. Undefined
d. Undefined

105. _____ is the extra revenue that an additional unit of product will bring a firm. It can also be described as the change in total revenue/change in number of units sold.
   a. Marginal revenue0
   b. Thing
   c. Undefined
   d. Undefined

106. A _____ is a negotiable instrument instructing a financial institution to pay a specific amount of a specific currency from a specific demand account held in the maker/depositor's name with that institution. Both the maker and payee may be natural persons or legal entities.
   a. Thing
   b. Check0
   c. Undefined
   d. Undefined

107. Fixed costs are expenses whose total does not change in proportion to the activity of a business.Unit fixed costs decline with volume following a retangular hyperbola as the volume of production.Variable costs by contrast change in relation to the activity of a business such as sales or production volume.Along with variable costs,fixed costs make up one of the two components of total cost. In the most simple production function total cost is equal to fixed costs plus variable costs.In accounting terminology, fixed costs will broadly include all costs which are not included in cost of goods sold, and variable costs are those captured in costs of goods sold. The implicit assumption required to make the equivalence between the accounting and economics terminology is that the accounting period is equal to the period in which fixed costs do not vary in relation to production. In practice, this equivalence does not always hold and depending on the period under consideration by management, some overhead expenses can be adjusted by management, and the specific allocation of each expense to each category will be decided under cost accounting.In business planning and management accounting, usage of the terms fixed costs, variable costs and others will often differ from usage in economics, and may depend on the intended use. For example, costs may be segregated into per unit costs fixed costs per period, and variable costs as a proportion of revenue. Capital expenditures will usually be allocated separately, and depending on the purpose, a portion may be regularly allocated to expenses as depreciation and amortization and seen as a _____ per period, or the entire amount may be considered upfront fixed costs.
   a. Fixed cost0
   b. Thing
   c. Undefined
   d. Undefined

108. _____ are expenses whose total does not change in proportion to the activity of a business, within the relevant time period or scale of production
   a. Thing
   b. Fixed costs0
   c. Undefined
   d. Undefined

109. A _____ is a symbolic representation denoting a quantity or expression. It often represents an "unknown" quantity that has the potential to change.
   a. Variable0
   b. Thing
   c. Undefined
   d. Undefined

110. Equivalence is the condition of being _____ or essentially equal.
   a. Thing
   b. Equivalent0
   c. Undefined
   d. Undefined

Chapter 4. USING THE DERIVATIVE

111. _____ asserts that the maximum output of a technologically-determined production process is a mathematical function of input factors of production.
   a. Production function0
   b. Thing
   c. Undefined
   d. Undefined

112. _____ is the application of tools and a processing medium to the transformation of raw materials into finished goods for sale.
   a. Thing
   b. Manufacturing0
   c. Undefined
   d. Undefined

113. In mathematics, a _____ is a quadric surface, with the following equation in Cartesian coordinates: $(x/_a)^2 + (y/_b)^2 = 1$.
   a. Thing
   b. Cylinder0
   c. Undefined
   d. Undefined

114. An _____ or member of a set is an object that when collected together make up the set.
   a. Thing
   b. Element0
   c. Undefined
   d. Undefined

115. In mathematics, the _____ , or members of a set or more generally a class are all those objects which when collected together make up the set or class.
   a. Thing
   b. Elements0
   c. Undefined
   d. Undefined

116. _____ is the transport of people on a trip/journey or the process or time involved in a person or object moving from one location to another.
   a. Thing
   b. Travel0
   c. Undefined
   d. Undefined

117. In combinatorial mathematics, a _____ is an un-ordered collection of unique elements.
   a. Combination0
   b. Concept
   c. Undefined
   d. Undefined

118. In geometry and trigonometry, a _____ is defined as an angle between two straight intersecting lines of ninety degrees, or one-quarter of a circle.
   a. Thing
   b. Right angle0
   c. Undefined
   d. Undefined

119. The _____ is a unit of plane angle. It is represented by the symbol "rad" or, more rarely, by the superscript c (for "circular measure"). For example, an angle of 1.2 radians would be written "1.2 rad" or "1.2c" (second symbol can produce confusion with centigrads).
   a. Thing
   b. Radian0
   c. Undefined
   d. Undefined

120. A _____ of a number is the product of that number with any integer.

Chapter 4. USING THE DERIVATIVE

    a. Multiple0
    b. Thing
    c. Undefined
    d. Undefined

121. In geometry, two lines or planes if one falls on the other in such a way as to create congruent adjacent angles. The term may be used as a noun or adjective. Thus, referring to Figure 1, the line AB is the _____ to CD through the point B.
    a. Perpendicular0
    b. Thing
    c. Undefined
    d. Undefined

122. In mathematics, a _____ is an algebraic structure in which addition and multiplication are defined and have properties listed below.
    a. Ring0
    b. Thing
    c. Undefined
    d. Undefined

123. In mathematics, a _____ is a two-dimensional manifold or surface that is perfectly flat.
    a. Plane0
    b. Thing
    c. Undefined
    d. Undefined

124. In geometry, a _____ is defined as a quadrilateral where all four of its angles are right angles.
    a. Thing
    b. Rectangle0
    c. Undefined
    d. Undefined

125. In geometry, a _____ is a special kind of point, usually a corner of a polygon, polyhedron, or higher dimensional polytope. In the geometry of curves a _____ is a point of where the first derivative of curvature is zero. In graph theory, a _____ is the fundamental unit out of which graphs are formed
    a. Thing
    b. Vertex0
    c. Undefined
    d. Undefined

126. _____ is the distance around a given two-dimensional object. As a general rule, the _____ of a polygon can always be calculated by adding all the length of the sides together. So, the formula for triangles is P = a + b + c, where a, b and c stand for each side of it. For quadrilaterals the equation is P = a + b + c + d. For equilateral polygons, P = na, where n is the number of sides and a is the side length.
    a. Thing
    b. Perimeter0
    c. Undefined
    d. Undefined

127. In mathematics, a _____ is the set of all points in three-dimensional space (R^3) which are at distance r from a fixed point of that space, where r is a positive real number called the radius of the _____. The fixed point is called the center or centre, and is not part of the _____ itself.
    a. Thing
    b. Sphere0
    c. Undefined
    d. Undefined

128. An _____ is a straight line around which a geometric figure can be rotated.
    a. Axis0
    b. Thing
    c. Undefined
    d. Undefined

129. _____ is electromagnetic radiation with a wavelength that is visible to the eye (visible _____) or, in a technical or scientific context, electromagnetic radiation of any wavelength.

Chapter 4. USING THE DERIVATIVE

    a. Thing
    b. Light0
    c. Undefined
    d. Undefined

130. A _____ is a three-dimensional solid object bounded by six square faces, facets, or sides, with three meeting at each vertex.
    a. Cube0
    b. Thing
    c. Undefined
    d. Undefined

131. _____ or arithmetics is the oldest and most elementary branch of mathematics, used by almost everyone, for tasks ranging from simple daily counting to advanced science and business calculations.
    a. Thing
    b. Arithmetic0
    c. Undefined
    d. Undefined

132. _____ of a list of numbers is the sum of all the members of the list divided by the number of items in the list.
    a. Thing
    b. Arithmetic mean0
    c. Undefined
    d. Undefined

133. In mathematics and more specifically set theory, the _____ set is the unique set which contains no elements.
    a. Empty0
    b. Thing
    c. Undefined
    d. Undefined

134. A _____ signifies a point or points of probability on a subject e.g., the _____ of creativity, which allows for the formation of rule or norm or law by interpretation of the phenomena events that can be created.
    a. Principle0
    b. Thing
    c. Undefined
    d. Undefined

135. A _____ given two distinct points A and B on the _____, is the set of points C on the line containing points A and B such that A is not strictly between C and B.
    a. Thing
    b. Ray0
    c. Undefined
    d. Undefined

136. A _____ is a quantity that denotes the proportional amount or magnitude of one quantity relative to another.
    a. Ratio0
    b. Thing
    c. Undefined
    d. Undefined

137. The word _____ is used in a variety of ways in mathematics.
    a. Index0
    b. Thing
    c. Undefined
    d. Undefined

138. In Euclidean geometry, a _____ is the set of all points in a plane at a fixed distance, called the radius, from a given point, the center.
    a. Circle0
    b. Thing
    c. Undefined
    d. Undefined

139. _____ is to give an equation $R(x,y) = S(x,y)$ that at least in part has the same graph as $y = f(x)$.

Chapter 4. USING THE DERIVATIVE

    a. Thing
    b. Implicit differentiation0
    c. Undefined
    d. Undefined

140. _____, a field in mathematics, is the study of how functions change when their inputs change. The primary object of study in _____ is the derivative.
    a. Differential calculus0
    b. Thing
    c. Undefined
    d. Undefined

141. A _____ consists of one quarter of the coordinate plane.
    a. Thing
    b. Quadrant0
    c. Undefined
    d. Undefined

142. In differential calculus, _____ problems involve finding the rate at which a quantity is changing by relating that quantity to other quantities whose rates of change are known.
    a. Related rates0
    b. Thing
    c. Undefined
    d. Undefined

143. In calculus, the _____ is a formula for the derivative of the composite of two functions.
    a. Chain rule0
    b. Concept
    c. Undefined
    d. Undefined

144. _____ is defined as the rate of change or derivative with respect to time of velocity.
    a. Thing
    b. Acceleration0
    c. Undefined
    d. Undefined

145. In Euclidean geometry, an _____ is a closed segment of a differentiable curve in the two-dimensional plane; for example, a circular _____ is a segment of a circle.
    a. Arc0
    b. Concept
    c. Undefined
    d. Undefined

146. _____ was an Greek philosopher. He is best known for a theorem in trigonometry that bears his name.
    a. Pythagoras0
    b. Person
    c. Undefined
    d. Undefined

147. In geometry, an _____ of a triangle is a straight line through a vertex and perpendicular to (i.e. forming a right angle with) the opposite side or an extension of the opposite side.
    a. Altitude0
    b. Concept
    c. Undefined
    d. Undefined

148. The _____ of a geographic location is its height above a fixed reference point, often the mean sea level.
    a. Elevation0
    b. Thing
    c. Undefined
    d. Undefined

149. _____ is a circle with a unit radius, i.e., a circle whose radius is 1.

Chapter 4. USING THE DERIVATIVE

    a. Thing
    c. Undefined
    b. Unit circle0
    d. Undefined

150. _____ is the difference of electrical potential between two points of an electrical or electronic circuit, expressed in volts
    a. Thing
    c. Undefined
    b. Voltage0
    d. Undefined

151. Sir Isaac _____, was an English physicist, mathematician, astronomer, natural philosopher, and alchemist, regarded by many as the greatest figure in the history of science
    a. Newton0
    c. Undefined
    b. Person
    d. Undefined

152. _____ is the weakest of the four fundamental forces of bature, as described by Issac Newton
    a. Thing
    c. Undefined
    b. Gravitational force0
    d. Undefined

153. A _____ is a vehicle, missile or aircraft which obtains thrust by the reaction to the ejection of fast moving fluid from within a _____ engine.
    a. Thing
    c. Undefined
    b. Rocket0
    d. Undefined

154. The deductive-nomological model is a formalized view of scientific _____ in natural language.
    a. Explanation0
    c. Undefined
    b. Thing
    d. Undefined

155. In mathematics, the _____ of two sets A and B is the set that contains all elements of A that also belong to B (or equivalently, all elements of B that also belong to A), but no other elements.
    a. Thing
    c. Undefined
    b. Intersection0
    d. Undefined

156. A _____ is a function that assigns a number to subsets of a given set.
    a. Thing
    c. Undefined
    b. Measure0
    d. Undefined

157. _____ is a special mathematical relationship between two quantities.Two quantities are called proportional if they vary in such a way that one of the quantities is a constant multiple of the other, or equivalently if they have a constant ratio.
    a. Thing
    c. Undefined
    b. Proportionality0
    d. Undefined

158. In mathematics, _____ growth occurs when the growth rate of a function is always proportional to the function's current size.
    a. Exponential0
    c. Undefined
    b. Thing
    d. Undefined

Chapter 4. USING THE DERIVATIVE

159. _____ is one of the most important functions in mathematics. A function commonly used to study growth and decay
   a. Exponential function0
   b. Thing
   c. Undefined
   d. Undefined

160. _____ has many meanings, most of which simply .
   a. Thing
   b. Power0
   c. Undefined
   d. Undefined

161. _____ statistics are statistics that estimate population parameters.
   a. Thing
   b. Parametric0
   c. Undefined
   d. Undefined

162. In mathematics, _____ bear slight similarity to functions: they allow one to use arbitrary values, called parameters, in place of independent variables in equations, which in turn provide values for dependent variables. A simple kinematical example is when one uses a time parameter to determine the position, velocity, and other information about a body in motion.
   a. Parametric equations0
   b. Thing
   c. Undefined
   d. Undefined

163. In linear algebra, the _____ of an n-by-n square matrix A is defined to be the sum of the elements on the main diagonal of A,
   a. Trace0
   b. Thing
   c. Undefined
   d. Undefined

164. In geometry, a line _____ is a part of a line that is bounded by two end points, and contains every point on the line between its end points.
   a. Segment0
   b. Concept
   c. Undefined
   d. Undefined

165. In mathematics, in the field of group theory, a _____ of a group is a quasisimple subnormal subgroup.
   a. Concept
   b. Component0
   c. Undefined
   d. Undefined

166. In business, particularly accounting, a _____ is the time intervals that the accounts, statement, payments, or other calculations cover.
   a. Thing
   b. Period0
   c. Undefined
   d. Undefined

167. _____ is a trigonemtric function that is important when studying triangles and modeling periodic phenomena, among other applications.
   a. Thing
   b. Sine0
   c. Undefined
   d. Undefined

168. Mathematical _____ are the wide variety of ways to capture an abstract mathematical concept or relationship.

Chapter 4. USING THE DERIVATIVE

   a. Representations0
   c. Undefined

   b. Thing
   d. Undefined

169. In mathematics, a _____ curve is the graph of the system of parametric equations, which describes complex harmonic motion.
   a. Lissajous0
   c. Undefined

   b. Thing
   d. Undefined

170. In mathematics, an _____ .
   a. Thing
   c. Undefined

   b. Ellipse0
   d. Undefined

171. A _____ is any object propelled through space by the applicationp of a force.
   a. Thing
   c. Undefined

   b. Projectile0
   d. Undefined

172. A _____ is 360° or 2ð radians.
   a. Thing
   c. Undefined

   b. Turn0
   d. Undefined

173. In _____ algebra, a *-ring is an associative ring with an antilinear, antiautomorphism * : A ¨ A which is an involution.
   a. Star0
   c. Undefined

   b. Thing
   d. Undefined

174. In physics, an _____ is the path that an object makes around another object while under the influence of a source of centripetal force, such as gravity.
   a. Orbit0
   c. Undefined

   b. Thing
   d. Undefined

175. A _____ , as defined by the International Astronomical Union , is a celestial body orbiting a star or stellar remnant that is massive enough to be rounded by its own gravity, not massive enough to cause thermonuclear fusion in its core, and has cleared its neighboring region of planetesimals.
   a. Thing
   c. Undefined

   b. Planet0
   d. Undefined

176. In mathematics, maxima and minima, known collectively as extrema, are the largest value maximum or smallest value minimum, that a function takes in a point either within a given neighborhood local _____ or on the function domain in its entirety global _____ .
   a. Thing
   c. Undefined

   b. Extremum0
   d. Undefined

177. The _____ in a vacuum is an important physical constant denoted by the letter c for constant or the Latin word celeritas meaning "swiftness

Chapter 4. USING THE DERIVATIVE

a. Thing
b. Speed of light0
c. Undefined
d. Undefined

178. A _____ is a method for fastening or securing linear material such as rope by tying or interweaving. It may consist of a length of one or more segments of rope, string, webbing, twine, strap or even chain interwoven so as to create in the line the ability to bind to itself or to some other object - the "load". Knots have been the subject of interest both for their ancient origins, common use, and the mathematical implications of _____ theory.
a. Knot0
b. Thing
c. Undefined
d. Undefined

179. A _____ is one of the basic shapes of geometry: a polygon with three vertices and three sides which are straight line segments.
a. Thing
b. Triangle0
c. Undefined
d. Undefined

180. _____ is the process of planning, recording, and controlling the movement of a craft or vehicle from one place to another.
a. Navigation0
b. Thing
c. Undefined
d. Undefined

181. _____ is the path a moving object follows through space.
a. Projectile motion0
b. Thing
c. Undefined
d. Undefined

182. _____ is the ability to hold, receive or absorb, or a measure thereof, similar to the concept of volume.
a. Concept
b. Capacity0
c. Undefined
d. Undefined

183. _____ usually refers to the biological _____ of a population level that can be supported for an organism, given the quantity of food, habitat, water and other life infrastructure present.
a. Thing
b. Carrying capacity0
c. Undefined
d. Undefined

184. _____ is a branch of mathematics concerning the study of structure, relation and quantity.
a. Algebra0
b. Concept
c. Undefined
d. Undefined

185. _____ element of an element x with respect to a binary operation * with identity element e is an element y such that x * y = y * x = e. In particular,
a. Thing
b. Inverse0
c. Undefined
d. Undefined

186. An _____ is a function which does the reverse of a given function.
a. Inverse function0
b. Thing
c. Undefined
d. Undefined

Chapter 4. USING THE DERIVATIVE

187. An _____ is an equality that remains true regardless of the values of any variables that appear within it, to distinguish it from an equality which is true under more particular conditions.
   a. Identity0
   b. Thing
   c. Undefined
   d. Undefined

188. In logic, and especially in its applications to mathematics and philosophy, a _____ is an exception to a proposed general rule, i.e., a specific instance of the falsity of a universal quantification (a "for all" statement).
   a. Thing
   b. Counterexample0
   c. Undefined
   d. Undefined

189. The _____ is the distance around a closed curve. _____ is a kind of perimeter.
   a. Circumference0
   b. Thing
   c. Undefined
   d. Undefined

190. _____ is a set, with some particular properties and usually some additional structure, such as the operations of addition or multiplication, for instance.
   a. Thing
   b. Space0
   c. Undefined
   d. Undefined

191. _____ is a professional society that focuses on undergraduate mathematics education.
   a. Mathematical Association of America0
   b. Person
   c. Undefined
   d. Undefined

192. A _____ is a compensation which workers receive in exchange for their labor.
   a. Wage0
   b. Thing
   c. Undefined
   d. Undefined

193. The payment of _____ as remuneration for services rendered or products sold is a common way to reward sales people.
   a. Thing
   b. Commission0
   c. Undefined
   d. Undefined

194. In mainstream economics, the word _____ refers to a general rise in prices measured against a standard level of purchasing power.
   a. Inflation0
   b. Thing
   c. Undefined
   d. Undefined

Chapter 5. KEY CONCEPT: THE DEFINITE INTEGRAL

1. _____ of an object is its speed in a particular direction.
   a. Thing
   b. Velocity0
   c. Undefined
   d. Undefined

2. _____ is a synonym for information.
   a. Thing
   b. Data0
   c. Undefined
   d. Undefined

3. In business, particularly accounting, a _____ is the time intervals that the accounts, statement, payments, or other calculations cover.
   a. Period0
   b. Thing
   c. Undefined
   d. Undefined

4. _____ is the transport of people on a trip/journey or the process or time involved in a person or object moving from one location to another.
   a. Thing
   b. Travel0
   c. Undefined
   d. Undefined

5. In mathematics, an inequality is a statement about the relative size or order of two objects. For example 14 > 10, or 14 is _____ 10.
   a. Thing
   b. Greater than0
   c. Undefined
   d. Undefined

6. _____ is the estimation of a physical quantity such as distance, energy, temperature, or time.
   a. Measurement0
   b. Thing
   c. Undefined
   d. Undefined

7. In elementary algebra, an _____ is a set that contains every real number between two indicated numbers and may contain the two numbers themselves.
   a. Thing
   b. Interval0
   c. Undefined
   d. Undefined

8. In geometry, a _____ is defined as a quadrilateral where all four of its angles are right angles.
   a. Thing
   b. Rectangle0
   c. Undefined
   d. Undefined

9. _____ is electromagnetic radiation with a wavelength that is visible to the eye (visible _____) or, in a technical or scientific context, electromagnetic radiation of any wavelength.
   a. Light0
   b. Thing
   c. Undefined
   d. Undefined

10. A _____ is the result of the addition of a set of numbers. The numbers may be natural numbers, complex numbers, matrices, or still more complicated objects. An infinite _____ is a subtle procedure known as a series.
    a. Sum0
    b. Thing
    c. Undefined
    d. Undefined

11. _____ is an extension of the concept of a sum.

a. Definite integral0 b. Thing
c. Undefined d. Undefined

12. The _____ of a function is an extension of the concept of a sum, and are identified or found through the use of integration.
   a. Thing b. Integral0
   c. Undefined d. Undefined

13. In mathematics, the concept of a _____ tries to capture the intuitive idea of a geometrical one-dimensional and continuous object. A simple example is the circle.
   a. Curve0 b. Thing
   c. Undefined d. Undefined

14. An _____ is a straight line around which a geometric figure can be rotated.
   a. Axis0 b. Thing
   c. Undefined d. Undefined

15. In astronomy, geography, geometry and related sciences and contexts, a plane is said to be _____ at a given point if it is locally perpendicular to the gradient of the gravity field, i.e., with the direction of the gravitational force at that point.
   a. Horizontal0 b. Thing
   c. Undefined d. Undefined

16. A _____ is one of the basic shapes of geometry: a polygon with three vertices and three sides which are straight line segments.
   a. Triangle0 b. Thing
   c. Undefined d. Undefined

17. In the scientific method, an _____ (Latin: ex-+-periri, "of (or from) trying"), is a set of actions and observations, performed in the context of solving a particular problem or question, in order to support or falsify a hypothesis or research concerning phenomena.
   a. Experiment0 b. Thing
   c. Undefined d. Undefined

18. Mathematical _____ is used to represent ideas.
   a. Notation0 b. Thing
   c. Undefined d. Undefined

19. The mathematical concept of a _____ expresses the intuitive idea of deterministic dependence between two quantities, one of which is viewed as primary and the other as secondary. A _____ then is a way to associate a unique output for each input of a specified type, for example, a real number or an element of a given set.
   a. Function0 b. Thing
   c. Undefined d. Undefined

20. An _____ is an increase, either of some fixed amount, for example added regularly, or of a variable amount.

Chapter 5. KEY CONCEPT: THE DEFINITE INTEGRAL

a. Thing
b. Increment0
c. Undefined
d. Undefined

21. The _____, the average in everyday English, which is also called the arithmetic _____ (and is distinguished from the geometric _____ or harmonic _____). The average is also called the sample _____. The expected value of a random variable, which is also called the population _____.
   a. Thing
   b. Mean0
   c. Undefined
   d. Undefined

22. _____ means in succession or back-to-back
   a. Thing
   b. Consecutive0
   c. Undefined
   d. Undefined

23. In mathematical analysis and related areas of mathematics, a set is called _____, if it is, in a certain sense, of finite size.
   a. Bounded0
   b. Thing
   c. Undefined
   d. Undefined

24. A _____ is a special kind of ratio, indicating a relationship between two measurements with different units, such as miles to gallons or cents to pounds.
   a. Rate0
   b. Thing
   c. Undefined
   d. Undefined

25. _____ are a measure of time.
   a. Thing
   b. Minutes0
   c. Undefined
   d. Undefined

26. In mathematics and the mathematical sciences, a _____ is a fixed, but possibly unspecified, value. This is in contrast to a variable, which is not fixed.
   a. Thing
   b. Constant0
   c. Undefined
   d. Undefined

27. _____ is defined as the rate of change or derivative with respect to time of velocity.
   a. Thing
   b. Acceleration0
   c. Undefined
   d. Undefined

28. A _____ is a unit of length, usually used to measure distance, in a number of different systems, including Imperial units, United States customary units and Norwegian/Swedish mil. Its size can vary from system to system, but in each is between 1 and 10 kilometers. In contemporary English contexts _____ refers to either:
   a. Mile0
   b. Thing
   c. Undefined
   d. Undefined

29. _____ is the eighteenth letter of the Greek alphabet.
   a. Sigma0
   b. Thing
   c. Undefined
   d. Undefined

Chapter 5. KEY CONCEPT: THE DEFINITE INTEGRAL

30. _____ is the addition of a set of numbers; the result is their sum. The "numbers" to be summed may be natural numbers, complex numbers, matrices, or still more complicated objects. An infinite sum is a subtle procedure known as a series.
    a. Summation0
    b. Thing
    c. Undefined
    d. Undefined

31. A _____ function is a function for which, intuitively, small changes in the input result in small changes in the output.
    a. Continuous0
    b. Event
    c. Undefined
    d. Undefined

32. _____ is a method for approximating the values of integrals.
    a. Thing
    b. Riemann sum0
    c. Undefined
    d. Undefined

33. In classical geometry, a _____ of a circle or sphere is any line segment from its center to its boundary. By extension, the _____ of a circle or sphere is the length of any such segment. The _____ is half the diameter. In science and engineering the term _____ of curvature is commonly used as a synonym for _____.
    a. Radius0
    b. Thing
    c. Undefined
    d. Undefined

34. In mathematics, the _____ is a conic section generated by the intersection of a right circular conical surface and a plane parallel to a generating straight line of that surface. It can also be defined as locus of points in a plane which are equidistant from a given point.
    a. Parabola0
    b. Thing
    c. Undefined
    d. Undefined

35. The act of _____ is the calculated approximation of a result which is usable even if input data may be incomplete, uncertain, or noisy.
    a. Thing
    b. Estimating0
    c. Undefined
    d. Undefined

36. The plus and _____ signs are mathematical symbols used to represent the notions of positive and negative as well as the operations of addition and subtraction.
    a. Thing
    b. Minus0
    c. Undefined
    d. Undefined

37. In geometry, an _____ is a point at which a line segment or ray terminates.
    a. Thing
    b. Endpoint0
    c. Undefined
    d. Undefined

38. In mathematics, the _____ f is the collection of all ordered pairs . In particular, graph means the graphical representation of this collection, in the form of a curve or surface, together with axes, etc. Graphing on a Cartesian plane is sometimes referred to as curve sketching.

Chapter 5. KEY CONCEPT: THE DEFINITE INTEGRAL

a. Graph of a function0
b. Thing
c. Undefined
d. Undefined

39. The _____ of measurement are a globally standardized and modernized form of the metric system.
   a. Units0
   b. Thing
   c. Undefined
   d. Undefined

40. A _____ is a quantity that denotes the proportional amount or magnitude of one quantity relative to another.
   a. Ratio0
   b. Thing
   c. Undefined
   d. Undefined

41. _____ was a German mathematician and philosopher. He invented calculus independently of Newton, and his notation is the one in general use since.
   a. Leibniz0
   b. Person
   c. Undefined
   d. Undefined

42. _____ named in honor of the 17th century German philosopher and mathematician Gottfried Wilhelm Leibniz, was originally the use of expressions such as dx and dy and to represent "infinitely small" or infinitesimal increments of quantities x and y, just as Äx and Äy represent finite increments of x and y respectively.
   a. Leibniz notation0
   b. Thing
   c. Undefined
   d. Undefined

43. In mathematics, a _____ is a statement that can be proved on the basis of explicitly stated or previously agreed assumptions.
   a. Theorem0
   b. Thing
   c. Undefined
   d. Undefined

44. The _____ is a measurement of how a function changes when the values of its inputs change.
   a. Derivative0
   b. Thing
   c. Undefined
   d. Undefined

45. In number theory, the _____ of arithmetic (or unique factorization theorem) states that every natural number greater than 1 can be written as a unique product of prime numbers.
   a. Fundamental theorem0
   b. Concept
   c. Undefined
   d. Undefined

46. In topology and related areas of mathematics a _____ or Moore-Smith sequence is a generalization of a sequence, intended to unify the various notions of limit and generalize them to arbitrary topological spaces.
   a. Thing
   b. Net0
   c. Undefined
   d. Undefined

47. In mathematics, a _____ is the result of multiplying, or an expression that identifies factors to be multiplied.
   a. Thing
   b. Product0
   c. Undefined
   d. Undefined

Chapter 5. KEY CONCEPT: THE DEFINITE INTEGRAL

48. _____ is a mathematical subject that includes the study of limits, derivatives, integrals, and power series and constitutes a major part of modern university curriculum.
   a. Thing
   b. Calculus0
   c. Undefined
   d. Undefined

49. _____ of calculus is the statement that the two central operations of calculus, differentiation and integration, are inverse operations: if a continuous function is first integrated and then differentiated, the original function is retrieved.
   a. Thing
   b. Fundamental Theorem of Calculus0
   c. Undefined
   d. Undefined

50. A _____ is a function that assigns a number to subsets of a given set.
   a. Measure0
   b. Thing
   c. Undefined
   d. Undefined

51. In sociology and biology a _____ is the collection of people or organisms of a particular species living in a given geographic area or space, usually measured by a census.
   a. Population0
   b. Thing
   c. Undefined
   d. Undefined

52. _____ generally, is the synthesis of triose phospates and ultimately starch, glucose and other products from sunlight, carbon dioxide and water.
   a. Thing
   b. Photosynthesis0
   c. Undefined
   d. Undefined

53. _____ is a kind of property which exists as magnitude or multitude. It is among the basic classes of things along with quality, substance, change, and relation.
   a. Amount0
   b. Thing
   c. Undefined
   d. Undefined

54. In mathematics, an _____, mean, or central tendency of a data set refers to a measure of the "middle" or "expected" value of the data set.
   a. Average0
   b. Concept
   c. Undefined
   d. Undefined

55. _____ is a physical property of a system that underlies the common notions of hot and cold; something that is hotter has the greater _____.
   a. Thing
   b. Temperature0
   c. Undefined
   d. Undefined

56. U.S. liquid _____ is legally defined as 231 cubic inches, and is equal to 3.785411784 litres or abotu 0.13368 cubic feet. This is the most common definition of a _____. The U.S. fluid ounce is defined as 1/128 of a U.S. _____.
   a. Gallon0
   b. Thing
   c. Undefined
   d. Undefined

Chapter 5. KEY CONCEPT: THE DEFINITE INTEGRAL

57. _____ is a set, with some particular properties and usually some additional structure, such as the operations of addition or multiplication, for instance.
   a. Space0
   b. Thing
   c. Undefined
   d. Undefined

58. In mathematics a _____ is a function which defines a distance between elements of a set.
   a. Metric0
   b. Thing
   c. Undefined
   d. Undefined

59. _____ are the basic objects of study in graph theory. Informally speaking, a graph is a set of objects called points, nodes, or vertices connected by links called lines or edges.
   a. Graphs0
   b. Thing
   c. Undefined
   d. Undefined

60. In mathematics, _____ are the intuitive idea of a geometrical one-dimensional and continuous object.
   a. Thing
   b. Curves0
   c. Undefined
   d. Undefined

61. A _____ is a function for which, intuitively, small changes in the input result in small changes in the output.
   a. Event
   b. Continuous function0
   c. Undefined
   d. Undefined

62. _____ is a process of combining or accumulating. It may also refer to:
   a. Integration0
   b. Thing
   c. Undefined
   d. Undefined

63. A _____ of a number is the product of that number with any integer.
   a. Thing
   b. Multiple0
   c. Undefined
   d. Undefined

64. _____ means "constancy", i.e. if something retains a certain feature even after we change a way of looking at it, then it is symmetric.
   a. Symmetry0
   b. Thing
   c. Undefined
   d. Undefined

65. _____ is a function that extends the concept of an ordinary sum
   a. Thing
   b. Integrand0
   c. Undefined
   d. Undefined

66. _____ are functions which satisfy particular symmetry relations, with respect to taking additive inverses.
   a. Thing
   b. Even function0
   c. Undefined
   d. Undefined

67. The metre (or _____, see spelling differences) is a measure of length. It is the basic unit of length in the metric system and in the International System of Units (SI), used around the world for general and scientific purposes.

Chapter 5. KEY CONCEPT: THE DEFINITE INTEGRAL

    a. Concept   b. Meter0
    c. Undefined   d. Undefined

68. The _____ of a solid object is the three-dimensional concept of how much space it occupies, often quantified numerically.
    a. Thing   b. Volume0
    c. Undefined   d. Undefined

69. The _____ (symbol _____) and the millibar (symbol mbar, also mb) are units of pressure.
    a. Thing   b. Bar0
    c. Undefined   d. Undefined

70. In Euclidean geometry, a uniform _____ is a linear transformation that enlargers or diminishes objects, and whose _____ factor is the same in all directions. This is also called homothety.
    a. Scale0   b. Thing
    c. Undefined   d. Undefined

71. Initial objects are also called _____, and terminal objects are also called final.
    a. Coterminal0   b. Thing
    c. Undefined   d. Undefined

72. An _____ is when two lines intersect somewhere on a plane creating a right angle at intersection
    a. Axes0   b. Thing
    c. Undefined   d. Undefined

73. In banking and accountancy, the outstanding _____ is the amount of money owned, or due, that remains in a deposit account or a loan account at a given date, after all past remittances, payments and withdrawal have been accounted for.
    a. Balance0   b. Thing
    c. Undefined   d. Undefined

74. In geometry, the _____ of an object is a point in some sense in the middle of the object.
    a. Thing   b. Center0
    c. Undefined   d. Undefined

75. The _____ of a mathematical object is its size: a property by which it can be larger or smaller than other objects of the same kind; in technical terms, an ordering of the class of objects to which it belongs.
    a. Magnitude0   b. Thing
    c. Undefined   d. Undefined

76. In geometry, an _____ of a triangle is a straight line through a vertex and perpendicular to (i.e. forming a right angle with) the opposite side or an extension of the opposite side.
    a. Concept   b. Altitude0
    c. Undefined   d. Undefined

77. In mathematics, there are several meanings of _____ depending on the subject.

Chapter 5. KEY CONCEPT: THE DEFINITE INTEGRAL

a. Thing
b. Degree0
c. Undefined
d. Undefined

78. In mathematics, a _____ is a countable collection of open covers of a topological space that satisfies certain separation axioms.
a. Thing
b. Development0
c. Undefined
d. Undefined

79. _____ is a branch of mathematics concerning the study of structure, relation and quantity.
a. Concept
b. Algebra0
c. Undefined
d. Undefined

80. An _____ is a combination of numbers, operators, grouping symbols and/or free variables and bound variables arranged in a meaningful way which can be evaluated..
a. Expression0
b. Thing
c. Undefined
d. Undefined

81. _____ is the state of being greater than any finite number, however large.
a. Thing
b. Infinity0
c. Undefined
d. Undefined

82. A _____ is a negotiable instrument instructing a financial institution to pay a specific amount of a specific currency from a specific demand account held in the maker/depositor's name with that institution. Both the maker and payee may be natural persons or legal entities.
a. Check0
b. Thing
c. Undefined
d. Undefined

83. In physics, an _____ is the path that an object makes around another object while under the influence of a source of centripetal force, such as gravity.
a. Thing
b. Orbit0
c. Undefined
d. Undefined

84. In computer science an _____ is a data structure that consists of a group of elements having a single name that are accessed by indexing. In most programming languages each element has the same data type and the _____ occupies a continuous area of storage.
a. Array0
b. Thing
c. Undefined
d. Undefined

85. _____ has many meanings, most of which simply .
a. Thing
b. Power0
c. Undefined
d. Undefined

86. _____ is the ability to hold, receive or absorb, or a measure thereof, similar to the concept of volume.
a. Concept
b. Capacity0
c. Undefined
d. Undefined

Chapter 5. KEY CONCEPT: THE DEFINITE INTEGRAL

87. The _____, in practice often shortened to amp, is a unit of electric current, or amount of electric charge per second.
    a. Thing
    b. Amperes0
    c. Undefined
    d. Undefined

88. In economics, supply and _____ describe market relations between prospective sellers and buyers of a good.
    a. Demand0
    b. Thing
    c. Undefined
    d. Undefined

89. _____ is the largest city in the state of Texas and the fourth-largest in the United States. As of the 2005 U.S. Census estimate, it had a population of more than 2 million.
    a. Thing
    b. Houston0
    c. Undefined
    d. Undefined

90. In mathematics, a _____ is a quadric surface, with the following equation in Cartesian coordinates: $(x/_a)^2 + (y/_b)^2 = 1$.
    a. Thing
    b. Cylinder0
    c. Undefined
    d. Undefined

91. In mathematics, the _____ of a coordinate system is the point where the axes of the system intersect.
    a. Origin0
    b. Thing
    c. Undefined
    d. Undefined

92. An _____ of a function f is a function F whose derivative is equal to f, i.e., F' = f.
    a. Antiderivative0
    b. Thing
    c. Undefined
    d. Undefined

Chapter 6. CONSTRUCTING ANTIDERIVATIVES

1. The _____ is a measurement of how a function changes when the values of its inputs change.
   a. Derivative0
   b. Thing
   c. Undefined
   d. Undefined

2. The mathematical concept of a _____ expresses the intuitive idea of deterministic dependence between two quantities, one of which is viewed as primary and the other as secondary. A _____ then is a way to associate a unique output for each input of a specified type, for example, a real number or an element of a given set.
   a. Function0
   b. Thing
   c. Undefined
   d. Undefined

3. _____ of an object is its speed in a particular direction.
   a. Thing
   b. Velocity0
   c. Undefined
   d. Undefined

4. Equivalence is the condition of being _____ or essentially equal.
   a. Equivalent0
   b. Thing
   c. Undefined
   d. Undefined

5. In mathematics and the mathematical sciences, a _____ is a fixed, but possibly unspecified, value. This is in contrast to a variable, which is not fixed.
   a. Constant0
   b. Thing
   c. Undefined
   d. Undefined

6. The _____, the average in everyday English, which is also called the arithmetic _____ (and is distinguished from the geometric _____ or harmonic _____). The average is also called the sample _____. The expected value of a random variable, which is also called the population _____.
   a. Thing
   b. Mean0
   c. Undefined
   d. Undefined

7. _____ is often used to describe the measurement of the steepness, incline, gradient, or grade of a straight line. The _____ is defined as the ratio of the "rise" divided by the "run" between two points on a line, or in other words, the ratio of the altitude change to the horizontal distance between any two points on the line.
   a. Slope0
   b. Thing
   c. Undefined
   d. Undefined

8. An _____ is a straight line around which a geometric figure can be rotated.
   a. Axis0
   b. Thing
   c. Undefined
   d. Undefined

9. Initial objects are also called _____, and terminal objects are also called final.
   a. Thing
   b. Coterminal0
   c. Undefined
   d. Undefined

10. _____ are the basic objects of study in graph theory. Informally speaking, a graph is a set of objects called points, nodes, or vertices connected by links called lines or edges.

a. Graphs0
b. Thing
c. Undefined
d. Undefined

11. In mathematics, the concept of a _____ tries to capture the intuitive idea of a geometrical one-dimensional and continuous object. A simple example is the circle.
   a. Curve0
   b. Thing
   c. Undefined
   d. Undefined

12. In mathematics, _____ are the intuitive idea of a geometrical one-dimensional and continuous object.
   a. Curves0
   b. Thing
   c. Undefined
   d. Undefined

13. In mathematics, in the field of differential equations, an initial value problem is a differential equation together with specified value, called the _____, of the unknown function at a given point in the domain of the solution.
   a. Initial condition0
   b. Thing
   c. Undefined
   d. Undefined

14. A real-valued function f defined on the real line is said to have a _____ point at the point x∗, if there exists some ε > 0, such that f when x − x∗ < ε.
   a. Thing
   b. Local maximum0
   c. Undefined
   d. Undefined

15. In mathematics, a _____ is a statement that can be proved on the basis of explicitly stated or previously agreed assumptions.
   a. Theorem0
   b. Thing
   c. Undefined
   d. Undefined

16. In number theory, the _____ of arithmetic (or unique factorization theorem) states that every natural number greater than 1 can be written as a unique product of prime numbers.
   a. Concept
   b. Fundamental theorem0
   c. Undefined
   d. Undefined

17. _____ is a point on the domain of a function
   a. Critical point0
   b. Thing
   c. Undefined
   d. Undefined

18. _____ is a a point on a curve at which the tangent crosses the curve itself.
   a. Inflection point0
   b. Thing
   c. Undefined
   d. Undefined

19. A _____ is a set of numbers that designate location in a given reference system, such as x,y in a planar _____ system or an x,y,z in a three-dimensional _____ system.
   a. Thing
   b. Coordinate0
   c. Undefined
   d. Undefined

20. _____ is an extension of the concept of a sum.

Chapter 6. CONSTRUCTING ANTIDERIVATIVES

    a. Definite integral0
    b. Thing
    c. Undefined
    d. Undefined

21. The _____ of a function is an extension of the concept of a sum, and are identified or found through the use of integration.
    a. Integral0
    b. Thing
    c. Undefined
    d. Undefined

22. A _____ is a special kind of ratio, indicating a relationship between two measurements with different units, such as miles to gallons or cents to pounds.
    a. Thing
    b. Rate0
    c. Undefined
    d. Undefined

23. _____ are a measure of time.
    a. Minutes0
    b. Thing
    c. Undefined
    d. Undefined

24. _____ is the level of functional and/or metabolic efficiency of an organism at both the micro level.
    a. Health0
    b. Thing
    c. Undefined
    d. Undefined

25. Acid _____ ratio measures the ability of a company to use its near cash or quick assets to immediately extinguish its current liabilities.
    a. Test0
    b. Thing
    c. Undefined
    d. Undefined

26. An _____ is when two lines intersect somewhere on a plane creating a right angle at intersection
    a. Thing
    b. Axes0
    c. Undefined
    d. Undefined

27. In trigonometry, the _____ is a function defined as $\tan x = \sin x / \cos x$. The function is so-named because it can be defined as the length of a certain segment of a _____ (in the geometric sense) to the unit circle. In plane geometry, a line is _____ to a curve, at some point, if both line and curve pass through the point with the same direction.
    a. Tangent0
    b. Thing
    c. Undefined
    d. Undefined

28. In astronomy, geography, geometry and related sciences and contexts, a plane is said to be _____ at a given point if it is locally perpendicular to the gradient of the gravity field, i.e., with the direction of the gravitational force at that point.
    a. Thing
    b. Horizontal0
    c. Undefined
    d. Undefined

29. _____ has two distinct but etymologically-related meanings: one in geometry and one in trigonometry.
    a. Tangent line0
    b. Thing
    c. Undefined
    d. Undefined

Chapter 6. CONSTRUCTING ANTIDERIVATIVES

30. In elementary algebra, an _____ is a set that contains every real number between two indicated numbers and may contain the two numbers themselves.
    a. Thing
    b. Interval0
    c. Undefined
    d. Undefined

31. In mathematics, a _____ is a demonstration that, assuming certain axioms, some statement is necessarily true.
    a. Proof0
    b. Thing
    c. Undefined
    d. Undefined

32. Mathematical _____ is used to represent ideas.
    a. Thing
    b. Notation0
    c. Undefined
    d. Undefined

33. _____ is a process of combining or accumulating. It may also refer to:
    a. Thing
    b. Integration0
    c. Undefined
    d. Undefined

34. In plane geometry, a _____ is a polygon with four equal sides, four right angles, and parallel opposite sides. In algebra, the _____ of a number is that number multiplied by itself.
    a. Square0
    b. Thing
    c. Undefined
    d. Undefined

35. In mathematics, a _____ of a number x is a number r such that $r^2 = x$, or in words, a number r whose square (the result of multiplying the number by itself) is x.
    a. Thing
    b. Square root0
    c. Undefined
    d. Undefined

36. In mathematics, a _____ of a complex-valued function f is a member x of the domain of f such that f(x) vanishes at x, that is, $x : f(x) = 0$.
    a. Root0
    b. Thing
    c. Undefined
    d. Undefined

37. A _____ is a negotiable instrument instructing a financial institution to pay a specific amount of a specific currency from a specific demand account held in the maker/depositor's name with that institution. Both the maker and payee may be natural persons or legal entities.
    a. Check0
    b. Thing
    c. Undefined
    d. Undefined

38. In common philosophical language, a proposition or _____, is the content of an assertion, that is, it is true-or-false and defined by the meaning of a particular piece of language.
    a. Concept
    b. Statement0
    c. Undefined
    d. Undefined

39. _____, a field in mathematics, is the study of how functions change when their inputs change. The primary object of study in _____ is the derivative.

Chapter 6. CONSTRUCTING ANTIDERIVATIVES

a. Thing
b. Differential calculus0
c. Undefined
d. Undefined

40. _____ is the logarithm to the base e, where e is an irrational constant approximately equal to 2.718281828459.
a. Natural logarithm0
b. Thing
c. Undefined
d. Undefined

41. In mathematics, a _____ of a number x is the exponent y of the power by such that $x = b^y$. The value used for the base b must be neither 0 nor 1, nor a root of 1 in the case of the extension to complex numbers, and is typically 10, e, or 2.
a. Thing
b. Logarithm0
c. Undefined
d. Undefined

42. A _____ is the result of the addition of a set of numbers. The numbers may be natural numbers, complex numbers, matrices, or still more complicated objects. An infinite _____ is a subtle procedure known as a series.
a. Sum0
b. Thing
c. Undefined
d. Undefined

43. _____ is a mathematical subject that includes the study of limits, derivatives, integrals, and power series and constitutes a major part of modern university curriculum.
a. Calculus0
b. Thing
c. Undefined
d. Undefined

44. _____ of calculus is the statement that the two central operations of calculus, differentiation and integration, are inverse operations: if a continuous function is first integrated and then differentiated, the original function is retrieved.
a. Fundamental Theorem of Calculus0
b. Thing
c. Undefined
d. Undefined

45. A _____ is traditionally an infinitesimally small change in a variable.
a. Thing
b. Differential0
c. Undefined
d. Undefined

46. The metre (or _____, see spelling differences) is a measure of length. It is the basic unit of length in the metric system and in the International System of Units (SI), used around the world for general and scientific purposes.
a. Meter0
b. Concept
c. Undefined
d. Undefined

47. In mathematics, an _____, mean, or central tendency of a data set refers to a measure of the "middle" or "expected" value of the data set.
a. Concept
b. Average0
c. Undefined
d. Undefined

48. In mathematics, the additive inverse, or _____ of a number n is the number that, when added to n, yields zero. The additive inverse of n is denoted −n. For example, 7 is −7, because 7 + (−7) = 0, and the additive inverse of −0.3 is 0.3, because −0.3 + 0.3 = 0.

Chapter 6. CONSTRUCTING ANTIDERIVATIVES

    a. Thing
    c. Undefined
    b. Opposite0
    d. Undefined

49. In mathematics, the _____ of a coordinate system is the point where the axes of the system intersect.
    a. Thing
    c. Undefined
    b. Origin0
    d. Undefined

50. In mathematics, the _____ of a number n is the number that, when added to n, yields zero. The _____ of n is denoted −n. For example, 7 is −7, because 7 + (−7) = 0, and the _____ of −0.3 is 0.3, because −0.3 + 0.3 = 0.
    a. Thing
    c. Undefined
    b. Additive inverse0
    d. Undefined

51. A _____ is a quantity that denotes the proportional amount or magnitude of one quantity relative to another.
    a. Thing
    c. Undefined
    b. Ratio0
    d. Undefined

52. A _____ is a mathematical equation for an unknown function of one or several variables which relates the values of the function itself and of its derivatives of various orders.
    a. Thing
    c. Undefined
    b. Differential equation0
    d. Undefined

53. _____ is defined as the rate of change or derivative with respect to time of velocity.
    a. Acceleration0
    c. Undefined
    b. Thing
    d. Undefined

54. A frame of _____ is a particular perspective from which the universe is observed.
    a. Reference0
    c. Undefined
    b. Thing
    d. Undefined

55. A _____ is a unit of length, usually used to measure distance, in a number of different systems, including Imperial units, United States customary units and Norwegian/Swedish mil. Its size can vary from system to system, but in each is between 1 and 10 kilometers. In contemporary English contexts _____ refers to either:
    a. Mile0
    c. Undefined
    b. Thing
    d. Undefined

56. _____ was an Italian physicist, mathematician, astronomer, and philosopher who is closely associated with the scientific revolution.
    a. Person
    c. Undefined
    b. Galileo Galilei0
    d. Undefined

57. The _____ of measurement are a globally standardized and modernized form of the metric system.
    a. Units0
    c. Undefined
    b. Thing
    d. Undefined

58. A _____ is a function that assigns a number to subsets of a given set.

Chapter 6. CONSTRUCTING ANTIDERIVATIVES

    a. Thing
    c. Undefined
    b. Measure0
    d. Undefined

59. A quadratic equation with real solutions, called roots, which may be real or complex, is given by the _____: $x = \frac{-b \pm \sqrt{b^2 - 4ac}}{2a}$.
    a. Quadratic formula0
    c. Undefined
    b. Thing
    d. Undefined

60. _____ is a differential equation together with specified value, called the initial condition, of the unknown function at a given point in the domain of the solution.
    a. Thing
    c. Undefined
    b. Initial value problem0
    d. Undefined

61. An _____ is a combination of numbers, operators, grouping symbols and/or free variables and bound variables arranged in a meaningful way which can be evaluated..
    a. Thing
    c. Undefined
    b. Expression0
    d. Undefined

62. _____ in calculus is primitive or indefinite integral of a function f is a function F whose derivative is equal to f, i.e., F Œ = f. The process of solving for antiderivatives is _____
    a. Antidifferentiation0
    c. Undefined
    b. Thing
    d. Undefined

63. A _____ function is a function for which, intuitively, small changes in the input result in small changes in the output.
    a. Continuous0
    c. Undefined
    b. Event
    d. Undefined

64. Compass and straightedge or ruler-and-compass _____ is the _____ of lengths or angles using only an idealized ruler and compass.
    a. Thing
    c. Undefined
    b. Construction0
    d. Undefined

65. In geometry, a _____ is defined as a quadrilateral where all four of its angles are right angles.
    a. Thing
    c. Undefined
    b. Rectangle0
    d. Undefined

66. In mathematics, there are several meanings of _____ depending on the subject.
    a. Thing
    c. Undefined
    b. Degree0
    d. Undefined

67. In mathematics, a _____ is the result of multiplying, or an expression that identifies factors to be multiplied.
    a. Thing
    c. Undefined
    b. Product0
    d. Undefined

68. The _____ governs the differentiation of products of differentiable functions.

Chapter 6. CONSTRUCTING ANTIDERIVATIVES

a. Thing
b. Product rule0
c. Undefined
d. Undefined

69. Sir Isaac _____, was an English physicist, mathematician, astronomer, natural philosopher, and alchemist, regarded by many as the greatest figure in the history of science
   a. Newton0
   b. Person
   c. Undefined
   d. Undefined

70. _____ was a Greek philosopher, a student of Plato and teacher of Alexander the Great. He wrote on diverse subjects, including physics, metaphysics, poetry, biology and zoology, logic, rhetoric, politics, government, and ethics.
   a. Person
   b. Aristotle0
   c. Undefined
   d. Undefined

71. _____, Greek for "knowledge of nature," is the branch of science concerned with the discovery and characterization of universal laws which govern matter, energy, space, and time.
   a. Thing
   b. Physics0
   c. Undefined
   d. Undefined

72. A _____ signifies a point or points of probability on a subject e.g., the _____ of creativity, which allows for the formation of rule or norm or law by interpretation of the phenomena events that can be created.
   a. Thing
   b. Principle0
   c. Undefined
   d. Undefined

73. In the scientific method, an _____ (Latin: ex-+-periri, "of (or from) trying"), is a set of actions and observations, performed in the context of solving a particular problem or question, in order to support or falsify a hypothesis or research concerning phenomena.
   a. Thing
   b. Experiment0
   c. Undefined
   d. Undefined

74. _____ is an adjective usually refering to being in the centre.
   a. Thing
   b. Central0
   c. Undefined
   d. Undefined

75. In physics, _____ is an influence that may cause an object to accelerate. It may be experienced as a lift, a push, or a pull. The actual acceleration of the body is determined by the vector sum of all forces acting on it, known as net _____ or resultant _____.
   a. Thing
   b. Force0
   c. Undefined
   d. Undefined

76. In topology and related areas of mathematics a _____ or Moore-Smith sequence is a generalization of a sequence, intended to unify the various notions of limit and generalize them to arbitrary topological spaces.
   a. Net0
   b. Thing
   c. Undefined
   d. Undefined

77. _____ is the property of a physical object that quantifies the amount of matter and energy it is equivalent to.

Chapter 6. CONSTRUCTING ANTIDERIVATIVES

a. Mass0
b. Thing
c. Undefined
d. Undefined

78. _____ is a vector produced when two or more forces act upon a single object.
a. Resultant force0
b. Thing
c. Undefined
d. Undefined

79. A _____ is a symbolic representation denoting a quantity or expression. It often represents an "unknown" quantity that has the potential to change.
a. Variable0
b. Thing
c. Undefined
d. Undefined

80. _____ is the weakest of the four fundamental forces of bature, as described by Issac Newton
a. Gravitational force0
b. Thing
c. Undefined
d. Undefined

81. In mathematics, two quantities are called _____ if they vary in such a way that one of the quantities is a constant multiple of the other, or equivalently if they have a constant ratio.
a. Thing
b. Proportional0
c. Undefined
d. Undefined

82. _____ is a set, with some particular properties and usually some additional structure, such as the operations of addition or multiplication, for instance.
a. Thing
b. Space0
c. Undefined
d. Undefined

83. _____ are objects, characters, or other concrete representations of ideas, concepts, or other abstractions.
a. Symbols0
b. Thing
c. Undefined
d. Undefined

84. In mathematical analysis and related areas of mathematics, a set is called _____, if it is, in a certain sense, of finite size.
a. Bounded0
b. Thing
c. Undefined
d. Undefined

85. In mathematics, the _____ is a conic section generated by the intersection of a right circular conical surface and a plane parallel to a generating straight line of that surface. It can also be defined as locus of points in a plane which are equidistant from a given point.
a. Parabola0
b. Thing
c. Undefined
d. Undefined

86. In mathematics, the _____ of two sets A and B is the set that contains all elements of A that also belong to B (or equivalently, all elements of B that also belong to A), but no other elements.
a. Thing
b. Intersection0
c. Undefined
d. Undefined

86 Chapter 6. CONSTRUCTING ANTIDERIVATIVES

87. _____ is a free computer algebra system based on a 1982 version of Macsyma
   a. Maxima0
   b. Thing
   c. Undefined
   d. Undefined

88. In mathematics, maxima and _____, known collectively as extrema, are points in the domain of a function at which the function takes a largest value .
   a. Thing
   b. Minima0
   c. Undefined
   d. Undefined

89. In physics, the _____ momentum of an object rotating about some reference point is the measure of the extent to which the object will continue to rotate about that point unless acted upon by an external torque.
   a. Thing
   b. Angular0
   c. Undefined
   d. Undefined

90. _____ is a scalar measure of rotation rate. It is the magnitude of the vector quantity angular velocity.
   a. Angular frequency0
   b. Thing
   c. Undefined
   d. Undefined

91. _____ is a scalar measure of rotation rate. It is the magnitude of the vector quantity angular velocity.
   a. Thing
   b. Angular speed0
   c. Undefined
   d. Undefined

92. _____ of a population is the number of childbirths per 1,000 persons per year
   a. Thing
   b. Birth rate0
   c. Undefined
   d. Undefined

93. In sociology and biology a _____ is the collection of people or organisms of a particular species living in a given geographic area or space, usually measured by a census.
   a. Thing
   b. Population0
   c. Undefined
   d. Undefined

94. _____ is a method for approximating the values of integrals.
   a. Riemann sum0
   b. Thing
   c. Undefined
   d. Undefined

95. _____ is a branch of mathematics concerning the study of structure, relation and quantity.
   a. Concept
   b. Algebra0
   c. Undefined
   d. Undefined

96. In mathematics, a _____ is a mathematical statement which appears likely to be true, but has not been formally proven to be true under the rules of mathematical logic.
   a. Concept
   b. Conjecture0
   c. Undefined
   d. Undefined

Chapter 6. CONSTRUCTING ANTIDERIVATIVES

97. In mathematics, a _____ is an expression that is constructed from one or more variables and constants, using only the operations of addition, subtraction, multiplication, and constant positive whole number exponents. is a _____. Note in particular that division by an expression containing a variable is not in general allowed in polynomials. [1]
   a. Thing
   b. Polynomial0
   c. Undefined
   d. Undefined

98. _____ is a function whose values do not vary and thus are constant.
   a. Thing
   b. Constant function0
   c. Undefined
   d. Undefined

99. In mathematical analysis, _____ are objects which generalize functions and probability distributions.
   a. Thing
   b. Distribution0
   c. Undefined
   d. Undefined

100. The word _____ is used in a variety of ways in mathematics.
   a. Thing
   b. Index0
   c. Undefined
   d. Undefined

101. In mathematics, an _____ is a statement about the relative size or order of two objects.
   a. Thing
   b. Inequality0
   c. Undefined
   d. Undefined

102. _____ is a business term for the amount of money that a company receives from its activities in a given period, mostly from sales of products and/or services to customers
   a. Revenue0
   b. Thing
   c. Undefined
   d. Undefined

Chapter 7. INTEGRATION

1. In mathematics, _____ is an elementary arithmetic operation. When one of the numbers is a whole number, _____ is the repeated sum of the other number.
   - a. Multiplication0
   - b. Thing
   - c. Undefined
   - d. Undefined

2. _____ is a process of combining or accumulating. It may also refer to:
   - a. Thing
   - b. Integration0
   - c. Undefined
   - d. Undefined

3. _____ is a tool for finding antiderivatives and integrals. Using the fundamental theorem of calculus often requires finding an antiderivative. For this and other reasons, this rule is a relatively important tool for mathematicians. It is the counterpart to the chain rule of differentiation.
   - a. Thing
   - b. Integration by substitution0
   - c. Undefined
   - d. Undefined

4. _____ has many meanings, most of which simply .
   - a. Thing
   - b. Power0
   - c. Undefined
   - d. Undefined

5. In mathematics, a _____ of a positive integer n is a way of writing n as a sum of positive integers.
   - a. Thing
   - b. Composition0
   - c. Undefined
   - d. Undefined

6. In mathematics and the mathematical sciences, a _____ is a fixed, but possibly unspecified, value. This is in contrast to a variable, which is not fixed.
   - a. Constant0
   - b. Thing
   - c. Undefined
   - d. Undefined

7. The mathematical concept of a _____ expresses the intuitive idea of deterministic dependence between two quantities, one of which is viewed as primary and the other as secondary. A _____ then is a way to associate a unique output for each input of a specified type, for example, a real number or an element of a given set.
   - a. Thing
   - b. Function0
   - c. Undefined
   - d. Undefined

8. An _____ of a function f is a function F whose derivative is equal to f, i.e., F' = f.
   - a. Antiderivative0
   - b. Thing
   - c. Undefined
   - d. Undefined

9. The _____ is a measurement of how a function changes when the values of its inputs change.
   - a. Derivative0
   - b. Thing
   - c. Undefined
   - d. Undefined

10. A _____ is a negotiable instrument instructing a financial institution to pay a specific amount of a specific currency from a specific demand account held in the maker/depositor's name with that institution. Both the maker and payee may be natural persons or legal entities.

Chapter 7. INTEGRATION

a. Check0
b. Thing
c. Undefined
d. Undefined

11. _____, a field in mathematics, is the study of how functions change when their inputs change. The primary object of study in _____ is the derivative.
   a. Differential calculus0
   b. Thing
   c. Undefined
   d. Undefined

12. _____ is a general method of problem solving for obtaining knowledge, both propositional and know-how. It is used typically in elementary algebra, when solving equations.
   a. Guess and check0
   b. Thing
   c. Undefined
   d. Undefined

13. In calculus, the _____ is a formula for the derivative of the composite of two functions.
   a. Chain rule0
   b. Concept
   c. Undefined
   d. Undefined

14. In mathematics, a _____ is the result of multiplying, or an expression that identifies factors to be multiplied.
   a. Thing
   b. Product0
   c. Undefined
   d. Undefined

15. In mathematics, factorization (British English: factorisation) or factoring is the decomposition of an object (for example, a number, a polynomial, or a matrix) into a product of other objects, or _____, which when multiplied together give the original.
   a. Thing
   b. Factors0
   c. Undefined
   d. Undefined

16. _____ is a trigonemtric function that is important when studying triangles and modeling periodic phenomena, among other applications.
   a. Thing
   b. Sine0
   c. Undefined
   d. Undefined

17. The _____ of an angle is the ratio of the length of the adjacent side to the length of the hypotenuse.
   a. Concept
   b. Cosine0
   c. Undefined
   d. Undefined

18. _____ is a function that extends the concept of an ordinary sum
   a. Thing
   b. Integrand0
   c. Undefined
   d. Undefined

19. A _____ is a symbolic representation denoting a quantity or expression. It often represents an "unknown" quantity that has the potential to change.
   a. Thing
   b. Variable0
   c. Undefined
   d. Undefined

Chapter 7. INTEGRATION

20. The _____ is used to discard one of the variables in an equation, only to replace it with the actual value when solving multiple equations.
    a. Substitution method0
    b. Thing
    c. Undefined
    d. Undefined

21. The _____ of a function is an extension of the concept of a sum, and are identified or found through the use of integration.
    a. Thing
    b. Integral0
    c. Undefined
    d. Undefined

22. _____ is an extension of the concept of a sum.
    a. Thing
    b. Definite integral0
    c. Undefined
    d. Undefined

23. In mathematics, a _____ is a statement that can be proved on the basis of explicitly stated or previously agreed assumptions.
    a. Thing
    b. Theorem0
    c. Undefined
    d. Undefined

24. _____ is a mathematical subject that includes the study of limits, derivatives, integrals, and power series and constitutes a major part of modern university curriculum.
    a. Calculus0
    b. Thing
    c. Undefined
    d. Undefined

25. In number theory, the _____ of arithmetic (or unique factorization theorem) states that every natural number greater than 1 can be written as a unique product of prime numbers.
    a. Fundamental theorem0
    b. Concept
    c. Undefined
    d. Undefined

26. _____ of calculus is the statement that the two central operations of calculus, differentiation and integration, are inverse operations: if a continuous function is first integrated and then differentiated, the original function is retrieved.
    a. Thing
    b. Fundamental Theorem of Calculus0
    c. Undefined
    d. Undefined

27. A _____ is 360° or 2δ radians.
    a. Turn0
    b. Thing
    c. Undefined
    d. Undefined

28. An _____ is a combination of numbers, operators, grouping symbols and/or free variables and bound variables arranged in a meaningful way which can be evaluated..
    a. Thing
    b. Expression0
    c. Undefined
    d. Undefined

29. In mathematics, a _____ of a complex-valued function f is a member x of the domain of f such that f(x) vanishes at x, that is, x : f (x) = 0.

Chapter 7. INTEGRATION

   a. Root0
   c. Undefined
   b. Thing
   d. Undefined

30. In mathematics, the concept of a _____ tries to capture the intuitive idea of a geometrical one-dimensional and continuous object. A simple example is the circle.
   a. Thing
   c. Undefined
   b. Curve0
   d. Undefined

31. In mathematics, the _____ functions are functions of an angle; they are important when studying triangles and modeling periodic phenomena, among many other applications.
   a. Trigonometric0
   c. Undefined
   b. Thing
   d. Undefined

32. _____ is defined as the rate of change or derivative with respect to time of velocity.
   a. Acceleration0
   c. Undefined
   b. Thing
   d. Undefined

33. The _____ governs the differentiation of products of differentiable functions.
   a. Product rule0
   c. Undefined
   b. Thing
   d. Undefined

34. In mathematics, a _____ is a constant multiplicative factor of a certain object. The object can be such things as a variable, a vector, a function, etc. For example, the _____ of $9x^2$ is 9.
   a. Coefficient0
   c. Undefined
   b. Thing
   d. Undefined

35. An _____ is an equality that remains true regardless of the values of any variables that appear within it, to distinguish it from an equality which is true under more particular conditions.
   a. Thing
   c. Undefined
   b. Identity0
   d. Undefined

36. In physics, _____ is the rate of change of acceleration; more precisely, the derivative of acceleration with respect to time, the second derivative of velocity, or the third derivative of displacement. _____ is described by the following equation:
   a. Jerk0
   c. Undefined
   b. Thing
   d. Undefined

37. A _____ is a special kind of ratio, indicating a relationship between two measurements with different units, such as miles to gallons or cents to pounds.
   a. Rate0
   c. Undefined
   b. Thing
   d. Undefined

38. In economics, supply and _____ describe market relations between prospective sellers and buyers of a good.
   a. Demand0
   c. Undefined
   b. Thing
   d. Undefined

39. A _____ is a function that assigns a number to subsets of a given set.
   a. Measure0
   b. Thing
   c. Undefined
   d. Undefined

40. In mathematics, a _____ is an expression that is constructed from one or more variables and constants, using only the operations of addition, subtraction, multiplication, and constant positive whole number exponents. is a _____. Note in particular that division by an expression containing a variable is not in general allowed in polynomials. [1]
   a. Polynomial0
   b. Thing
   c. Undefined
   d. Undefined

41. In mathematics, _____ refers to the rewriting of an expression into a simpler form.
   a. Reduction0
   b. Thing
   c. Undefined
   d. Undefined

42. In mathematics, there are several meanings of _____ depending on the subject.
   a. Thing
   b. Degree0
   c. Undefined
   d. Undefined

43. _____ is a mathematical operation, written a^n, involving two numbers, the base a and the exponent n.
   a. Exponentiating0
   b. Thing
   c. Undefined
   d. Undefined

44. _____ is a mathematical operation, written a^n, involving two numbers, the base a and the exponent n.
   a. Exponentiation0
   b. Thing
   c. Undefined
   d. Undefined

45. In plane geometry, a _____ is a polygon with four equal sides, four right angles, and parallel opposite sides. In algebra, the _____ of a number is that number multiplied by itself.
   a. Thing
   b. Square0
   c. Undefined
   d. Undefined

46. In mathematics, _____ is the decomposition of an object into a product of other objects, or factors, which when multiplied together give the original.
   a. Factoring0
   b. Thing
   c. Undefined
   d. Undefined

47. _____ is a technique used in algebra to solve quadratic equations, in analytic geometry for determining the shapes of graphs, and in calculus for computing integrals, including, but hardly limited to, the integrals that define Laplace transforms. The essential objective is to reduce a quadratic polynomial in a variable in an equation or expression to a squared polynomial of linear order. This can reduce an equation or integral to one that is more easily solved or evaluated.
   a. Thing
   b. Completing the square0
   c. Undefined
   d. Undefined

48. In arithmetic, _____ is a procedure for calculating the division of one integer, called the dividend, by another integer called the divisor, to produce a result called the quotient.

Chapter 7. INTEGRATION

a. Thing
b. Long division0
c. Undefined
d. Undefined

49. In mathematics, an inequality is a statement about the relative size or order of two objects. For example 14 > 10, or 14 is _____ 10.
   a. Greater than0
   b. Thing
   c. Undefined
   d. Undefined

50. A _____ is a numeral used to indicate a count. The most common use of the word today is to name the part of a fraction that tells the number or count of equal parts.
   a. Thing
   b. Numerator0
   c. Undefined
   d. Undefined

51. In mathematics, a _____ number is a number which can be expressed as a ratio of two integers. Non-integer _____ numbers (commonly called fractions) are usually written as the vulgar fraction a / b, where b is not zero.
   a. Thing
   b. Rational0
   c. Undefined
   d. Undefined

52. In mathematics, a _____ is any function which can be written as the ratio of two polynomial functions.
   a. Thing
   b. Rational function0
   c. Undefined
   d. Undefined

53. A _____ is the part of a fraction that tells how many equal parts make up a whole, and which is used in the name of the fraction: "halves", "thirds", "fourths" or "quarters", "fifths" and so on.
   a. Denominator0
   b. Concept
   c. Undefined
   d. Undefined

54. The _____ are the only integral domain whose positive elements are well-ordered, and in which order is preserved by addition. Like the natural numbers, the _____ form a countably infinite set. The set of all _____ is usually denoted in mathematics by a boldface Z .
   a. Thing
   b. Integers0
   c. Undefined
   d. Undefined

55. _____ is the difference of electrical potential between two points of an electrical or electronic circuit, expressed in volts
   a. Thing
   b. Voltage0
   c. Undefined
   d. Undefined

56. In mathematics, an _____, mean, or central tendency of a data set refers to a measure of the "middle" or "expected" value of the data set.
   a. Average0
   b. Concept
   c. Undefined
   d. Undefined

57. In economics, economic _____ is simply a state of the world where economic forces are balanced and in the absence of external influences the values of economic variables will not change.

94 *Chapter 7. INTEGRATION*

   a. Thing
   c. Undefined
   b. Equilibrium0
   d. Undefined

58. _____ is a kind of property which exists as magnitude or multitude. It is among the basic classes of things along with quality, substance, change, and relation.
   a. Amount0
   c. Undefined
   b. Thing
   d. Undefined

59. In mathematics, _____ is the substitution of trigonometric functions for other expressions.
   a. Thing
   c. Undefined
   b. Trigonometric substitution0
   d. Undefined

60. In algebra, the _____ decomposition or _____ expansion is used to reduce the degree of either the numerator or the denominator of a rational function.
   a. Partial fraction0
   c. Undefined
   b. Thing
   d. Undefined

61. _____ is a fixed, but possibly unspecified, value. This is in contrast to a variable, which is not fixed.
   a. Thing
   c. Undefined
   b. Constant term0
   d. Undefined

62. The word _____ comes from the Latin word linearis, which means created by lines.
   a. Thing
   c. Undefined
   b. Linear0
   d. Undefined

63. _____ is the property of two events happening at the same time in at least one reference frame.
   a. Simultaneous0
   c. Undefined
   b. Thing
   d. Undefined

64. _____ traditionally refers to the statistical process of determining comparable scores on different forms of an exam
   a. Thing
   c. Undefined
   b. Equating0
   d. Undefined

65. _____ are a set of equations containing multiple variables.
   a. Thing
   c. Undefined
   b. Systems of equations0
   d. Undefined

66. A _____ is the part of the dividend that is left over when the dividend is not evenly divisible by the divisor.
   a. Thing
   c. Undefined
   b. Remainder0
   d. Undefined

67. In mathematics, a _____ of a number x is a number r such that $r^2 = x$, or in words, a number r whose square (the result of multiplying the number by itself) is x.

Chapter 7. INTEGRATION

    a. Thing
    b. Square root0
    c. Undefined
    d. Undefined

68. In elementary algebra, an _____ is a set that contains every real number between two indicated numbers and may contain the two numbers themselves.
    a. Interval0
    b. Thing
    c. Undefined
    d. Undefined

69. In statistics, a _____ measure is one which is measuring what is supposed to measure.
    a. Valid0
    b. Thing
    c. Undefined
    d. Undefined

70. In mathematics, the _____ of a function is the set of all "output" values produced by that function. Given a function $f : A \to B$, the _____ of f, is defined to be the set $\{x \in B : x = f(a) \text{ for some } a \in A\}$.
    a. Range0
    b. Thing
    c. Undefined
    d. Undefined

71. _____ element of an element x with respect to a binary operation * with identity element e is an element y such that x * y = y * x = e. In particular,
    a. Inverse0
    b. Thing
    c. Undefined
    d. Undefined

72. In mathematics, a _____ of a k-place relation $L \subseteq X_1 \times \ldots \times X_k$ is one of the sets X_j, $1 \leq j \leq k$. In the special case where k = 2 and $L \subseteq X_1 \times X_2$ is a function $L : X_1 \to X_2$, it is conventional to refer to X_1 as the _____ of the function and to refer to X_2 as the codomain of the function.
    a. Domain0
    b. Thing
    c. Undefined
    d. Undefined

73. In mathematics, an _____ .
    a. Ellipse0
    b. Thing
    c. Undefined
    d. Undefined

74. In mathematics, a _____ is a type of conic section defined as the intersection between a right circular conical surface and a plane which cuts through both halves of the cone.
    a. Thing
    b. Hyperbola0
    c. Undefined
    d. Undefined

75. In trigonometry, the _____ is a function defined as $\tan x = \sin x / \cos x$. The function is so-named because it can be defined as the length of a certain segment of a _____ (in the geometric sense) to the unit circle. In plane geometry, a line is _____ to a curve, at some point, if both line and curve pass through the point with the same direction.
    a. Tangent0
    b. Thing
    c. Undefined
    d. Undefined

76. In linear algebra, a _____ of a matrix A is the determinant of some smaller square matrix, cut down from A.

a. Minor0
b. Thing
c. Undefined
d. Undefined

77. In mathematics, the _____(e) for L-functions are a class of summation formulae, expressing sums taken over the complex number zeroes of a given L-function, typically in terms of quantities studied by number theory by use of the theory of special functions.
a. Thing
b. Explicit formula0
c. Undefined
d. Undefined

78. _____ is a way of expressing a number as a fraction of 100 per cent meaning "per hundred".
a. Percent0
b. Thing
c. Undefined
d. Undefined

79. In sociology and biology a _____ is the collection of people or organisms of a particular species living in a given geographic area or space, usually measured by a census.
a. Thing
b. Population0
c. Undefined
d. Undefined

80. A _____ is the result of the addition of a set of numbers. The numbers may be natural numbers, complex numbers, matrices, or still more complicated objects. An infinite _____ is a subtle procedure known as a series.
a. Sum0
b. Thing
c. Undefined
d. Undefined

81. In geometry, an _____ is a point at which a line segment or ray terminates.
a. Thing
b. Endpoint0
c. Undefined
d. Undefined

82. In geometry, a _____ is defined as a quadrilateral where all four of its angles are right angles.
a. Rectangle0
b. Thing
c. Undefined
d. Undefined

83. _____ is a method for approximating the values of integrals.
a. Thing
b. Riemann sum0
c. Undefined
d. Undefined

84. _____ is the middle point of a line segment.
a. Thing
b. Midpoint0
c. Undefined
d. Undefined

85. The act of _____ is the calculated approximation of a result which is usable even if input data may be incomplete, uncertain, or noisy.
a. Thing
b. Estimating0
c. Undefined
d. Undefined

86. A _____ is a quadrilateral, which is defined as a shape with four sides, which has a pair of parallel sides.

a. Thing
b. Trapezoid0
c. Undefined
d. Undefined

87. The word _____ means curving in or hollowed inward.
   a. Concavity0
   b. Thing
   c. Undefined
   d. Undefined

88. A _____ is one of the basic shapes of geometry: a polygon with three vertices and three sides which are straight line segments.
   a. Thing
   b. Triangle0
   c. Undefined
   d. Undefined

89. In geometry, two sets are called _____ if one can be transformed into the other by an isometry, i.e., a combination of translations, rotations and reflections.
   a. Congruent0
   b. Thing
   c. Undefined
   d. Undefined

90. A circular _____ or circle _____ also known as a pie piece is the portion of a circle enclosed by two radii and an arc.
   a. Thing
   b. Sector0
   c. Undefined
   d. Undefined

91. In Euclidean geometry, a _____ is the set of all points in a plane at a fixed distance, called the radius, from a given point, the center.
   a. Circle0
   b. Thing
   c. Undefined
   d. Undefined

92. _____ has one 90° internal angle a right angle.
   a. Thing
   b. Right triangle0
   c. Undefined
   d. Undefined

93. In mathematics, especially in order theory, an _____ of a subset S of some partially ordered set is an element of P which is greater than or equal to every element of S.
   a. Upper bound0
   b. Thing
   c. Undefined
   d. Undefined

94. A _____ is a deliberate process for transforming one or more inputs into one or more results.
   a. Thing
   b. Calculation0
   c. Undefined
   d. Undefined

95. The _____ function (weight function) is a mathematical device used when performing a sum, integral, or average in order to give some elements more of a "weight" than others.
   a. Thing
   b. Weighted0
   c. Undefined
   d. Undefined

96. A _____ is often used in statistics.

a. Weighted mean0   b. Thing
c. Undefined   d. Undefined

97. In mathematics, the additive inverse, or _____ of a number n is the number that, when added to n, yields zero. The additive inverse of n is denoted −n. For example, 7 is −7, because 7 + (−7) = 0, and the additive inverse of −0.3 is 0.3, because −0.3 + 0.3 = 0.
   a. Thing   b. Opposite0
   c. Undefined   d. Undefined

98. The _____ of a mathematical object is its size: a property by which it can be larger or smaller than other objects of the same kind; in technical terms, an ordering of the class of objects to which it belongs.
   a. Thing   b. Magnitude0
   c. Undefined   d. Undefined

99. In mathematics, the _____ of a number n is the number that, when added to n, yields zero. The _____ of n is denoted −n. For example, 7 is −7, because 7 + (−7) = 0, and the _____ of −0.3 is 0.3, because −0.3 + 0.3 = 0.
   a. Additive inverse0   b. Thing
   c. Undefined   d. Undefined

100. A central concept in science and the scientific method is that all evidence must be _____, or empirically based, that is, dependent on evidence or consequences that are observable by the senses.
   a. Thing   b. Empirical0
   c. Undefined   d. Undefined

101. A _____ is a first degree polynomial mathematical function of the form: f(x) = mx + b where m and b are real constants and x is a real variable.
   a. Linear function0   b. Thing
   c. Undefined   d. Undefined

102. A _____ is a polynomial function of the form f(x) = ax^2 + bx +c , where a, b, c are real numbers and a ≠ 0.
   a. Event   b. Quadratic function0
   c. Undefined   d. Undefined

103. An _____ is the limit of a definite integral, as an endpoint of the interval of integration approaches either a specified real number or ‡ or − ‡ or, in some cases, as both endpoints approach limits.
   a. Improper integral0 b. Thing
   c. Undefined   d. Undefined

104. In mathematics, a set is called _____ if there is a bijection between the set and some set of the form {1, 2, ..., n} where n is a natural number.
   a. Finite0   b. Thing
   c. Undefined   d. Undefined

105. _____ is the state of being greater than any finite number, however large.

Chapter 7. INTEGRATION

a. Infinity0   b. Thing
c. Undefined   d. Undefined

106. _____ is the SI unit of energy.
a. Thing   b. Joule0
c. Undefined   d. Undefined

107. The metre (or _____, see spelling differences) is a measure of length. It is the basic unit of length in the metric system and in the International System of Units (SI), used around the world for general and scientific purposes.
a. Concept   b. Meter0
c. Undefined   d. Undefined

108. Initial objects are also called _____, and terminal objects are also called final.
a. Thing   b. Coterminal0
c. Undefined   d. Undefined

109. _____ is the state of being greater than any finite real or natural number, however large.
a. Infinite0   b. Thing
c. Undefined   d. Undefined

110. _____ is a straight line or curve A to which another curve B the one being studied approaches closer and closer as one moves along it.
a. Thing   b. Vertical asymptote0
c. Undefined   d. Undefined

111. An _____ is a straight line or curve A to which another curve B approaches closer and closer as one moves along it. As one moves along B, the space between it and the _____ A becomes smaller and smaller, and can in fact be made as small as one could wish by going far enough along. A curve may or may not touch or cross its _____. In fact, the curve may intersect the _____ an infinite number of times.
a. Asymptote0   b. Thing
c. Undefined   d. Undefined

112. _____ denotes the approach toward a definite value, as time goes on; or to a definite point, a common view or opinion, or toward a fixed or equilibrium state.
a. Convergence0   b. Thing
c. Undefined   d. Undefined

113. In mathematics, defined and _____ are used to explain whether or not expressions have meaningful, sensible, and unambiguous values.
a. Undefined0   b. Thing
c. Undefined   d. Undefined

114. The _____, also called Gaussian distribution by scientists, is a continuous probability distribution of great importance in many fields.

Chapter 7. INTEGRATION

a. Normal distribution0
b. Thing
c. Undefined
d. Undefined

115. In mathematical analysis, _____ are objects which generalize functions and probability distributions.
a. Distribution0
b. Thing
c. Undefined
d. Undefined

116. In mathematics, _____ describes an entity with a limit.
a. Convergent0
b. Thing
c. Undefined
d. Undefined

117. In epidemiology, an _____ is a disease that appears as new cases in a given human population, during a given period, at a rate that substantially exceeds with is "expected," based on recent experience.
a. Epidemic0
b. Thing
c. Undefined
d. Undefined

118. In mathematics, an _____ is a statement about the relative size or order of two objects.
a. Thing
b. Inequality0
c. Undefined
d. Undefined

119. The _____, the average in everyday English, which is also called the arithmetic _____ (and is distinguished from the geometric _____ or harmonic _____). The average is also called the sample _____. The expected value of a random variable, which is also called the population _____.
a. Thing
b. Mean0
c. Undefined
d. Undefined

120. _____ is an operator that measures the magnitude of a vector field's source or sink at a given point; the _____ of a vector field is a signed scalar.
a. Thing
b. Divergence0
c. Undefined
d. Undefined

121. Acid _____ ratio measures the ability of a company to use its near cash or quick assets to immediately extinguish its current liabilities.
a. Test0
b. Thing
c. Undefined
d. Undefined

122. _____ is a criterion for convergence or divergence of a series whose terms are real or complex numbers.
a. Comparison test0
b. Thing
c. Undefined
d. Undefined

123. _____ has two distinct but etymologically-related meanings: one in geometry and one in trigonometry.
a. Thing
b. Tangent line0
c. Undefined
d. Undefined

124. In mathematics, _____ are the intuitive idea of a geometrical one-dimensional and continuous object.

Chapter 7. INTEGRATION

a. Curves0
b. Thing
c. Undefined
d. Undefined

125. _____ are the basic objects of study in graph theory. Informally speaking, a graph is a set of objects called points, nodes, or vertices connected by links called lines or edges.
   a. Thing
   b. Graphs0
   c. Undefined
   d. Undefined

126. In mathematics, a _____ section is a curve that can be formed by intersecting a cone with a plane.
   a. Conic0
   b. Thing
   c. Undefined
   d. Undefined

127. _____ is a mathematical science pertaining to the collection, analysis, interpretation or explanation, and presentation of data. It is applicable to a wide variety of academic disciplines, from the physical and social sciences to the humanities.
   a. Statistics0
   b. Thing
   c. Undefined
   d. Undefined

128. In mathematics a _____ is a formal power series whose coefficients encode information about a sequence a_n that is indexed by the natural numbers.
   a. Thing
   b. Generating function0
   c. Undefined
   d. Undefined

129. _____ is a physical property of a system that underlies the common notions of hot and cold; something that is hotter has the greater _____.
   a. Temperature0
   b. Thing
   c. Undefined
   d. Undefined

130. In mathematics, a _____ is a countable collection of open covers of a topological space that satisfies certain separation axioms.
   a. Thing
   b. Development0
   c. Undefined
   d. Undefined

131. _____ is a branch of mathematics concerning the study of structure, relation and quantity.
   a. Concept
   b. Algebra0
   c. Undefined
   d. Undefined

132. A _____ function is a function for which, intuitively, small changes in the input result in small changes in the output.
   a. Event
   b. Continuous0
   c. Undefined
   d. Undefined

133. In common philosophical language, a proposition or _____, is the content of an assertion, that is, it is true-or-false and defined by the meaning of a particular piece of language.

a. Concept
b. Statement0
c. Undefined
d. Undefined

134. _____ is a function whose values do not vary and thus are constant.
   a. Thing
   b. Constant function0
   c. Undefined
   d. Undefined

135. _____ is the logarithm to the base e, where e is an irrational constant approximately equal to 2.718281828459.
   a. Natural logarithm0
   b. Thing
   c. Undefined
   d. Undefined

136. In mathematics, a _____ of a number x is the exponent y of the power by such that $x = b^y$. The value used for the base b must be neither 0 nor 1, nor a root of 1 in the case of the extension to complex numbers, and is typically 10, e, or 2.
   a. Thing
   b. Logarithm0
   c. Undefined
   d. Undefined

137. A _____ is a function that repeats its values after some definite period has been added to its independent variable.
   a. Thing
   b. Periodic function0
   c. Undefined
   d. Undefined

138. In Euclidean geometry, an _____ is a closed segment of a differentiable curve in the two-dimensional plane; for example, a circular _____ is a segment of a circle.
   a. Arc0
   b. Concept
   c. Undefined
   d. Undefined

139. _____ is often used to describe the measurement of the steepness, incline, gradient, or grade of a straight line. The _____ is defined as the ratio of the "rise" divided by the "run" between two points on a line, or in other words, the ratio of the altitude change to the horizontal distance between any two points on the line.
   a. Slope0
   b. Thing
   c. Undefined
   d. Undefined

140. In geometry, a line _____ is a part of a line that is bounded by two end points, and contains every point on the line between its end points.
   a. Concept
   b. Segment0
   c. Undefined
   d. Undefined

141. A _____ is a part of a line that is bounded by two end points, and contains every point on the line between its end points.
   a. Line segment0
   b. Thing
   c. Undefined
   d. Undefined

142. In mathematics, a _____ is a two-dimensional manifold or surface that is perfectly flat.
   a. Thing
   b. Plane0
   c. Undefined
   d. Undefined

Chapter 7. INTEGRATION

143. A _____ is a graphical tool to qualitatively visualize, or aid in numerical approximation of, solutions to differential equations.
   a. Thing
   b. Slope field0
   c. Undefined
   d. Undefined

144. In mathematics, the _____ is a conic section generated by the intersection of a right circular conical surface and a plane parallel to a generating straight line of that surface. It can also be defined as locus of points in a plane which are equidistant from a given point.
   a. Parabola0
   b. Thing
   c. Undefined
   d. Undefined

145. In linear algebra, the _____ of an n-by-n square matrix A is defined to be the sum of the elements on the main diagonal of A,
   a. Thing
   b. Trace0
   c. Undefined
   d. Undefined

Chapter 8. USING THE DEFINITE INTEGRAL

1. The _____ of a solid object is the three-dimensional concept of how much space it occupies, often quantified numerically.
   a. Volume0
   b. Thing
   c. Undefined
   d. Undefined

2. _____ is an extension of the concept of a sum.
   a. Definite integral0
   b. Thing
   c. Undefined
   d. Undefined

3. The _____ of a function is an extension of the concept of a sum, and are identified or found through the use of integration.
   a. Integral0
   b. Thing
   c. Undefined
   d. Undefined

4. A _____ is the result of the addition of a set of numbers. The numbers may be natural numbers, complex numbers, matrices, or still more complicated objects. An infinite _____ is a subtle procedure known as a series.
   a. Sum0
   b. Thing
   c. Undefined
   d. Undefined

5. _____ is a method for approximating the values of integrals.
   a. Thing
   b. Riemann sum0
   c. Undefined
   d. Undefined

6. A _____ is one of the basic shapes of geometry: a polygon with three vertices and three sides which are straight line segments.
   a. Triangle0
   b. Thing
   c. Undefined
   d. Undefined

7. A _____ is a negotiable instrument instructing a financial institution to pay a specific amount of a specific currency from a specific demand account held in the maker/depositor's name with that institution. Both the maker and payee may be natural persons or legal entities.
   a. Thing
   b. Check0
   c. Undefined
   d. Undefined

8. In astronomy, geography, geometry and related sciences and contexts, a plane is said to be _____ at a given point if it is locally perpendicular to the gradient of the gravity field, i.e., with the direction of the gravitational force at that point.
   a. Thing
   b. Horizontal0
   c. Undefined
   d. Undefined

9. _____ is a process of combining or accumulating. It may also refer to:
   a. Integration0
   b. Thing
   c. Undefined
   d. Undefined

10. An _____ triange is a triangle with at least two sides of equal length.
    a. Isosceles0
    b. Thing
    c. Undefined
    d. Undefined

Chapter 8. USING THE DEFINITE INTEGRAL

11. In geometry, a _____ is defined as a quadrilateral where all four of its angles are right angles.
    a. Thing
    b. Rectangle0
    c. Undefined
    d. Undefined

12. A _____ is a symbolic representation denoting a quantity or expression. It often represents an "unknown" quantity that has the potential to change.
    a. Variable0
    b. Thing
    c. Undefined
    d. Undefined

13. In mathematics, _____ geometry was the traditional name for the geometry of three-dimensional Euclidean space — for practical purposes the kind of space we live in.
    a. Solid0
    b. Thing
    c. Undefined
    d. Undefined

14. In geometry, a _____ is a special kind of point, usually a corner of a polygon, polyhedron, or higher dimensional polytope. In the geometry of curves a _____ is a point of where the first derivative of curvature is zero. In graph theory, a _____ is the fundamental unit out of which graphs are formed
    a. Vertex0
    b. Thing
    c. Undefined
    d. Undefined

15. A _____ is a three-dimensional geometric shape formed by straight lines through a fixed point (vertex) to the points of a fixed curve (directrix)
    a. Cone0
    b. Concept
    c. Undefined
    d. Undefined

16. In classical geometry, a _____ of a circle or sphere is any line segment from its center to its boundary. By extension, the _____ of a circle or sphere is the length of any such segment. The _____ is half the diameter. In science and engineering the term _____ of curvature is commonly used as a synonym for _____.
    a. Radius0
    b. Thing
    c. Undefined
    d. Undefined

17. In mathematics, a _____ is a quadric surface, with the following equation in Cartesian coordinates: $(x/_a)^2 + (y/_b)^2 = 1$.
    a. Thing
    b. Cylinder0
    c. Undefined
    d. Undefined

18. In Euclidean geometry, a _____ is the set of all points in a plane at a fixed distance, called the radius, from a given point, the center.
    a. Circle0
    b. Thing
    c. Undefined
    d. Undefined

19. In geometry, the _____ of an object is a point in some sense in the middle of the object.
    a. Center0
    b. Thing
    c. Undefined
    d. Undefined

Chapter 8. USING THE DEFINITE INTEGRAL

20. In mathematics, a _____ is the set of all points in three-dimensional space (R^3) which are at distance r from a fixed point of that space, where r is a positive real number called the radius of the _____. The fixed point is called the center or centre, and is not part of the _____ itself.
   a. Sphere0
   b. Thing
   c. Undefined
   d. Undefined

21. An n-sided _____ is a polyhedron formed by connecting an n-sided polygonal base and a point, called the apex, by n triangular faces. In other words, it is a conic solid with polygonal base.
   a. Thing
   b. Pyramid0
   c. Undefined
   d. Undefined

22. In plane geometry, a _____ is a polygon with four equal sides, four right angles, and parallel opposite sides. In algebra, the _____ of a number is that number multiplied by itself.
   a. Thing
   b. Square0
   c. Undefined
   d. Undefined

23. The mathematical concept of a _____ expresses the intuitive idea of deterministic dependence between two quantities, one of which is viewed as primary and the other as secondary. A _____ then is a way to associate a unique output for each input of a specified type, for example, a real number or an element of a given set.
   a. Thing
   b. Function0
   c. Undefined
   d. Undefined

24. A _____ is a function that assigns a number to subsets of a given set.
   a. Thing
   b. Measure0
   c. Undefined
   d. Undefined

25. In geometry, a _____ is the intersection of a body in 2-dimensional space with a line, or of a body in 3-dimensional space with a plane
   a. Thing
   b. Cross section0
   c. Undefined
   d. Undefined

26. In Euclidean geometry, a uniform _____ is a linear transformation that enlargers or diminishes objects, and whose _____ factor is the same in all directions. This is also called homothethy.
   a. Thing
   b. Scale0
   c. Undefined
   d. Undefined

27. The metre (or _____, see spelling differences) is a measure of length. It is the basic unit of length in the metric system and in the International System of Units (SI), used around the world for general and scientific purposes.
   a. Concept
   b. Meter0
   c. Undefined
   d. Undefined

28. An _____ is a straight line around which a geometric figure can be rotated.
   a. Axis0
   b. Thing
   c. Undefined
   d. Undefined

Chapter 8. USING THE DEFINITE INTEGRAL

29. In mathematics, the concept of a _____ tries to capture the intuitive idea of a geometrical one-dimensional and continuous object. A simple example is the circle.
    a. Thing
    b. Curve0
    c. Undefined
    d. Undefined

30. In mathematics, _____ are the intuitive idea of a geometrical one-dimensional and continuous object.
    a. Thing
    b. Curves0
    c. Undefined
    d. Undefined

31. In geometry, two lines or planes if one falls on the other in such a way as to create congruent adjacent angles. The term may be used as a noun or adjective. Thus, referring to Figure 1, the line AB is the _____ to CD through the point B.
    a. Thing
    b. Perpendicular0
    c. Undefined
    d. Undefined

32. In mathematical analysis and related areas of mathematics, a set is called _____, if it is, in a certain sense, of finite size.
    a. Thing
    b. Bounded0
    c. Undefined
    d. Undefined

33. _____ was an Greek philosopher. He is best known for a theorem in trigonometry that bears his name.
    a. Person
    b. Pythagoras0
    c. Undefined
    d. Undefined

34. In mathematics, a _____ is a statement that can be proved on the basis of explicitly stated or previously agreed assumptions.
    a. Theorem0
    b. Thing
    c. Undefined
    d. Undefined

35. In Euclidean geometry, an _____ is a closed segment of a differentiable curve in the two-dimensional plane; for example, a circular _____ is a segment of a circle.
    a. Concept
    b. Arc0
    c. Undefined
    d. Undefined

36. _____ also called rectification of a curve—was historically difficult.
    a. Arc length0
    b. Thing
    c. Undefined
    d. Undefined

37. _____ is a function that extends the concept of an ordinary sum
    a. Thing
    b. Integrand0
    c. Undefined
    d. Undefined

38. An _____ of a function f is a function F whose derivative is equal to f, i.e., F' = f.
    a. Antiderivative0
    b. Thing
    c. Undefined
    d. Undefined

39. An _____ is when two lines intersect somewhere on a plane creating a right angle at intersection

a. Thing
b. Axes0
c. Undefined
d. Undefined

40. _____ statistics are statistics that estimate population parameters.
a. Thing
b. Parametric0
c. Undefined
d. Undefined

41. In mathematics, _____ bear slight similarity to functions: they allow one to use arbitrary values, called parameters, in place of independent variables in equations, which in turn provide values for dependent variables. A simple kinematical example is when one uses a time parameter to determine the position, velocity, and other information about a body in motion.
a. Thing
b. Parametric equations0
c. Undefined
d. Undefined

42. In mathematics, a _____ is a two-dimensional manifold or surface that is perfectly flat.
a. Thing
b. Plane0
c. Undefined
d. Undefined

43. _____ is the transport of people on a trip/journey or the process or time involved in a person or object moving from one location to another.
a. Thing
b. Travel0
c. Undefined
d. Undefined

44. In mathematics, an _____ .
a. Thing
b. Ellipse0
c. Undefined
d. Undefined

45. The _____ is the distance around a closed curve. _____ is a kind of perimeter.
a. Circumference0
b. Thing
c. Undefined
d. Undefined

46. An _____ is a type of quadric surface that is a higher dimensional analogue of an ellipse.
a. Ellipsoid0
b. Thing
c. Undefined
d. Undefined

47. In geometry, an _____ polygon is a polygon which has all sides of the same length.
a. Equilateral0
b. Thing
c. Undefined
d. Undefined

48. An _____ is a triangle in which all sides are of equal length.
a. Equilateral triangle0
b. Thing
c. Undefined
d. Undefined

49. A _____ signifies a point or points of probability on a subject e.g., the _____ of creativity, which allows for the formation of rule or norm or law by interpretation of the phenomena events that can be created.

Chapter 8. USING THE DEFINITE INTEGRAL

a. Thing
b. Principle0
c. Undefined
d. Undefined

50. _____ of Syracuse was an ancient Greek mathematician, physicist and engineer. In addition to making important discoveries in the field of mathematics and geometry, he is credited with producing machines that were well ahead of their time.
   a. Archimedes0
   b. Person
   c. Undefined
   d. Undefined

51. In physics, _____ is an influence that may cause an object to accelerate. It may be experienced as a lift, a push, or a pull. The actual acceleration of the body is determined by the vector sum of all forces acting on it, known as net _____ or resultant _____.
   a. Thing
   b. Force0
   c. Undefined
   d. Undefined

52. In mathematics, two quantities are called _____ if they vary in such a way that one of the quantities is a constant multiple of the other, or equivalently if they have a constant ratio.
   a. Thing
   b. Proportional0
   c. Undefined
   d. Undefined

53. _____ is a special mathematical relationship between two quantities. Two quantities are called proportional if they vary in such a way that one of the quantities is a constant multiple of the other, or equivalently if they have a constant ratio.
   a. Thing
   b. Proportionality0
   c. Undefined
   d. Undefined

54. The _____ of measurement are a globally standardized and modernized form of the metric system.
   a. Thing
   b. Units0
   c. Undefined
   d. Undefined

55. A _____ is a special kind of ratio, indicating a relationship between two measurements with different units, such as miles to gallons or cents to pounds.
   a. Rate0
   b. Thing
   c. Undefined
   d. Undefined

56. In mathematics and the mathematical sciences, a _____ is a fixed, but possibly unspecified, value. This is in contrast to a variable, which is not fixed.
   a. Constant0
   b. Thing
   c. Undefined
   d. Undefined

57. In mathematics and more specifically set theory, the _____ set is the unique set which contains no elements.
   a. Empty0
   b. Thing
   c. Undefined
   d. Undefined

58. _____ the American term is a way to approximately calculate the definite integral

Chapter 8. USING THE DEFINITE INTEGRAL

   a. Thing
   c. Undefined
   b. Trapezoidal Rule0
   d. Undefined

59. _____ is the distance around a given two-dimensional object. As a general rule, the _____ of a polygon can always be calculated by adding all the length of the sides together. So, the formula for triangles is P = a + b + c, where a, b and c stand for each side of it. For quadrilaterals the equation is P = a + b + c + d. For equilateral polygons, P = na, where n is the number of sides and a is the side length.
   a. Thing
   c. Undefined
   b. Perimeter0
   d. Undefined

60. _____ is the shape of a hanging flexible chain or cable when supported at its ends and acted upon by a uniform gravitational force. The chain is steepest near the points of suspension because this part of the chain has the most weight pulling down on it. Toward the bottom, the slope of the chain decreases because the chain is supporting less weight.
   a. Catenary0
   c. Undefined
   b. Thing
   d. Undefined

61. _____ in calculus is primitive or indefinite integral of a function f is a function F whose derivative is equal to f, i.e., F Œ = f. The process of solving for antiderivatives is _____
   a. Antidifferentiation0
   c. Undefined
   b. Thing
   d. Undefined

62. A _____ is a set of numbers that designate location in a given reference system, such as x,y in a planar _____ system or an x,y,z in a three-dimensional _____ system.
   a. Coordinate0
   c. Undefined
   b. Thing
   d. Undefined

63. In functional analysis and related areas of mathematics the _____ set of a given subset of a vector space is a certain set in the dual space.
   a. Thing
   c. Undefined
   b. Polar0
   d. Undefined

64. _____ means of or relating to the French philosopher and mathematician RenÃ© Descartes.
   a. Thing
   c. Undefined
   b. Cartesian0
   d. Undefined

65. In mathematics, the _____ of a coordinate system is the point where the axes of the system intersect.
   a. Thing
   c. Undefined
   b. Origin0
   d. Undefined

66. A _____ consists of one quarter of the coordinate plane.
   a. Thing
   c. Undefined
   b. Quadrant0
   d. Undefined

67. _____ has one 90° internal angle a right angle.

a. Thing
b. Right triangle0
c. Undefined
d. Undefined

68. The _____ is a unit of plane angle. It is represented by the symbol "rad" or, more rarely, by the superscript c (for "circular measure"). For example, an angle of 1.2 radians would be written "1.2 rad" or "1.2c" (second symbol can produce confusion with centigrads).
   a. Thing
   b. Radian0
   c. Undefined
   d. Undefined

69. _____ are the basic objects of study in graph theory. Informally speaking, a graph is a set of objects called points, nodes, or vertices connected by links called lines or edges.
   a. Graphs0
   b. Thing
   c. Undefined
   d. Undefined

70. _____ is a circle with a unit radius, i.e., a circle whose radius is 1.
   a. Thing
   b. Unit circle0
   c. Undefined
   d. Undefined

71. In linear algebra, the _____ of an n-by-n square matrix A is defined to be the sum of the elements on the main diagonal of A,
   a. Thing
   b. Trace0
   c. Undefined
   d. Undefined

72. In mathematics, the additive inverse, or _____ of a number n is the number that, when added to n, yields zero. The additive inverse of n is denoted −n. For example, 7 is −7, because 7 + (−7) = 0, and the additive inverse of −0.3 is 0.3, because −0.3 + 0.3 = 0.
   a. Thing
   b. Opposite0
   c. Undefined
   d. Undefined

73. In computer programs, an important form of control flow is the _____.
   a. Thing
   b. Inner loop0
   c. Undefined
   d. Undefined

74. In mathematics, the _____ of a number n is the number that, when added to n, yields zero. The _____ of n is denoted −n. For example, 7 is −7, because 7 + (−7) = 0, and the _____ of −0.3 is 0.3, because −0.3 + 0.3 = 0.
   a. Thing
   b. Additive inverse0
   c. Undefined
   d. Undefined

75. In mathematics, an _____ is a statement about the relative size or order of two objects.
   a. Thing
   b. Inequality0
   c. Undefined
   d. Undefined

76. In mathematics, a subset of Euclidean space R^n is called _____ if it is closed and bounded.
   a. Compact0
   b. Thing
   c. Undefined
   d. Undefined

77. In geometry, a _____ (Greek words diairo = divide and metro = measure) of a circle is any straight line segment that passes through the centre and whose endpoints are on the circular boundary, or, in more modern usage, the length of such a line segment. When using the word in the more modern sense, one speaks of the _____ rather than a _____, because all diameters of a circle have the same length. This length is twice the radius. The _____ of a circle is also the longest chord that the circle has.
  a. Diameter0
  b. Thing
  c. Undefined
  d. Undefined

78. A circular _____ or circle _____ also known as a pie piece is the portion of a circle enclosed by two radii and an arc.
  a. Sector0
  b. Thing
  c. Undefined
  d. Undefined

79. In mathematics, a _____ is a heart-shaped mathematical curve. The cardioid is considered a special case, with a cusp.
  a. Thing
  b. Limagon0
  c. Undefined
  d. Undefined

80. Two mathematical objects are equal if and only if they are precisely the same in every way. This defines a binary relation, _____, denoted by the sign of _____ "=" in such a way that the statement "x = y" means that x and y are equal.
  a. Equality0
  b. Thing
  c. Undefined
  d. Undefined

81. In mathematics, a _____ are a curve which emanates from a central point, getting progressively farther away as it revolves around the point.
  a. Spirals0
  b. Thing
  c. Undefined
  d. Undefined

82. In geometry, the _____ is an epicycloid with one cusp. That is, a _____ is a curve that can be produced as the path of a point on the circumference of a circle as that circle rolls around another fixed circle with the same radius.
  a. Thing
  b. Cardioid0
  c. Undefined
  d. Undefined

83. In mathematics, the _____ of Bernoulli is an eight-shaped algebraic curve described by a Cartesian equation
  a. Thing
  b. Lemniscate0
  c. Undefined
  d. Undefined

84. In trigonometry, the _____ is a function defined as tan x = $^{\sin x}/_{\cos x}$. The function is so-named because it can be defined as the length of a certain segment of a _____ (in the geometric sense) to the unit circle. In plane geometry, a line is _____ to a curve, at some point, if both line and curve pass through the point with the same direction.
  a. Tangent0
  b. Thing
  c. Undefined
  d. Undefined

Chapter 8. USING THE DEFINITE INTEGRAL

85. An _____ is a straight line or curve A to which another curve B approaches closer and closer as one moves along it. As one moves along B, the space between it and the _____ A becomes smaller and smaller, and can in fact be made as small as one could wish by going far enough along. A curve may or may not touch or cross its _____. In fact, the curve may intersect the _____ an infinite number of times.
   a. Thing
   b. Asymptote0
   c. Undefined
   d. Undefined

86. _____ has two distinct but etymologically-related meanings: one in geometry and one in trigonometry.
   a. Thing
   b. Tangent line0
   c. Undefined
   d. Undefined

87. _____ is the property of a physical object that quantifies the amount of matter and energy it is equivalent to.
   a. Thing
   b. Mass0
   c. Undefined
   d. Undefined

88. _____ is mass m per unit volume V.
   a. Density0
   b. Thing
   c. Undefined
   d. Undefined

89. In sociology and biology a _____ is the collection of people or organisms of a particular species living in a given geographic area or space, usually measured by a census.
   a. Thing
   b. Population0
   c. Undefined
   d. Undefined

90. A _____ is a unit of length, usually used to measure distance, in a number of different systems, including Imperial units, United States customary units and Norwegian/Swedish mil. Its size can vary from system to system, but in each is between 1 and 10 kilometers. In contemporary English contexts _____ refers to either:
   a. Mile0
   b. Thing
   c. Undefined
   d. Undefined

91. In geometry, a line _____ is a part of a line that is bounded by two end points, and contains every point on the line between its end points.
   a. Concept
   b. Segment0
   c. Undefined
   d. Undefined

92. In elementary algebra, an _____ is a set that contains every real number between two indicated numbers and may contain the two numbers themselves.
   a. Interval0
   b. Thing
   c. Undefined
   d. Undefined

93. A _____ is a unit of length in the metric system, equal to one thousand metres, the current SI base unit of length
   a. Thing
   b. Kilometer0
   c. Undefined
   d. Undefined

94. In mathematics, a matrix can be thought of as each row or _____ being a vector. Hence, a space formed by row vectors or _____ vectors are said to be a row space or a _____ space.

a. Column0
b. Concept
c. Undefined
d. Undefined

95. In geometry, an _____ of a triangle is a straight line through a vertex and perpendicular to (i.e. forming a right angle with) the opposite side or an extension of the opposite side.
   a. Altitude0
   b. Concept
   c. Undefined
   d. Undefined

96. In mathematics, a _____ is an algebraic structure in which addition and multiplication are defined and have properties listed below.
   a. Thing
   b. Ring0
   c. Undefined
   d. Undefined

97. An _____ is a combination of numbers, operators, grouping symbols and/or free variables and bound variables arranged in a meaningful way which can be evaluated..
   a. Expression0
   b. Thing
   c. Undefined
   d. Undefined

98. In banking and accountancy, the outstanding _____ is the amount of money owned, or due, that remains in a deposit account or a loan account at a given date, after all past remittances, payments and withdrawal have been accounted for.
   a. Balance0
   b. Thing
   c. Undefined
   d. Undefined

99. A _____ is 360° or 2ð radians.
   a. Turn0
   b. Thing
   c. Undefined
   d. Undefined

100. In physics, the _____ of a system of particles is a specific point at which, for many purposes, the system's mass behaves as if it were concentrated.
   a. Thing
   b. Center of mass0
   c. Undefined
   d. Undefined

101. A _____ is the part of a fraction that tells how many equal parts make up a whole, and which is used in the name of the fraction: "halves", "thirds", "fourths" or "quarters", "fifths" and so on.
   a. Denominator0
   b. Concept
   c. Undefined
   d. Undefined

102. The word _____ comes from the 15th Century Latin word discretus which means separate.
   a. Thing
   b. Discrete0
   c. Undefined
   d. Undefined

103. In mathematics, a _____ is an n-tuple with n being 3.
   a. Triple0
   b. Thing
   c. Undefined
   d. Undefined

Chapter 8. USING THE DEFINITE INTEGRAL

104. _____ is a mathematical subject that includes the study of limits, derivatives, integrals, and power series and constitutes a major part of modern university curriculum.
   a. Thing
   b. Calculus0
   c. Undefined
   d. Undefined

105. _____ means "constancy", i.e. if something retains a certain feature even after we change a way of looking at it, then it is symmetric.
   a. Thing
   b. Symmetry0
   c. Undefined
   d. Undefined

106. _____ is electromagnetic radiation with a wavelength that is visible to the eye (visible _____) or, in a technical or scientific context, electromagnetic radiation of any wavelength.
   a. Light0
   b. Thing
   c. Undefined
   d. Undefined

107. In mathematics, _____ growth occurs when the growth rate of a function is always proportional to the function's current size.
   a. Thing
   b. Exponential0
   c. Undefined
   d. Undefined

108. _____ is a physical property of a system that underlies the common notions of hot and cold; something that is hotter has the greater _____ .
   a. Thing
   b. Temperature0
   c. Undefined
   d. Undefined

109. In mathematics, an inequality is a statement about the relative size or order of two objects. For example 14 > 10, or 14 is _____ 10.
   a. Thing
   b. Greater than0
   c. Undefined
   d. Undefined

110. _____ of an object is its speed in a particular direction.
   a. Velocity0
   b. Thing
   c. Undefined
   d. Undefined

111. Sir Isaac _____ , was an English physicist, mathematician, astronomer, natural philosopher, and alchemist, regarded by many as the greatest figure in the history of science
   a. Newton0
   b. Person
   c. Undefined
   d. Undefined

112. _____ , Greek for "knowledge of nature," is the branch of science concerned with the discovery and characterization of universal laws which govern matter, energy, space, and time.
   a. Thing
   b. Physics0
   c. Undefined
   d. Undefined

113. _____ has many meanings, most of which simply .

Chapter 8. USING THE DEFINITE INTEGRAL

   a. Thing
   c. Undefined
   b. Power0
   d. Undefined

114. In mathematics, a _____ is a countable collection of open covers of a topological space that satisfies certain separation axioms.
   a. Development0
   c. Undefined
   b. Thing
   d. Undefined

115. _____ is the SI unit of energy.
   a. Joule0
   c. Undefined
   b. Thing
   d. Undefined

116. An _____ is an increase, either of some fixed amount, for example added regularly, or of a variable amount.
   a. Increment0
   c. Undefined
   b. Thing
   d. Undefined

117. _____ is the weakest of the four fundamental forces of bature, as described by Issac Newton
   a. Thing
   c. Undefined
   b. Gravitational force0
   d. Undefined

118. _____ is defined as the rate of change or derivative with respect to time of velocity.
   a. Thing
   c. Undefined
   b. Acceleration0
   d. Undefined

119. The _____ or kilogramme is the SI base unit of mass. It is defined as being equal to the mass of the international prototype of the _____.
   a. Kilogram0
   c. Undefined
   b. Thing
   d. Undefined

120. _____ is a set, with some particular properties and usually some additional structure, such as the operations of addition or multiplication, for instance.
   a. Thing
   c. Undefined
   b. Space0
   d. Undefined

121. _____ is a kind of property which exists as magnitude or multitude. It is among the basic classes of things along with quality, substance, change, and relation.
   a. Amount0
   c. Undefined
   b. Thing
   d. Undefined

122. Compass and straightedge or ruler-and-compass _____ is the _____ of lengths or angles using only an idealized ruler and compass.
   a. Thing
   c. Undefined
   b. Construction0
   d. Undefined

123. In business, particularly accounting, a _____ is the time intervals that the accounts, statement, payments, or other calculations cover.

Chapter 8. USING THE DEFINITE INTEGRAL

a. Thing
b. Period0
c. Undefined
d. Undefined

124. _____ is the pressure at some point withig the fluid
    a. Water pressure0
    b. Thing
    c. Undefined
    d. Undefined

125. A _____ is a quadrilateral, which is defined as a shape with four sides, which has a pair of parallel sides.
    a. Trapezoid0
    b. Thing
    c. Undefined
    d. Undefined

126. _____ is often used to describe the measurement of the steepness, incline, gradient, or grade of a straight line. The _____ is defined as the ratio of the "rise" divided by the "run" between two points on a line, or in other words, the ratio of the altitude change to the horizontal distance between any two points on the line.
    a. Slope0
    b. Thing
    c. Undefined
    d. Undefined

127. The word _____ comes from the Latin word linearis, which means created by lines.
    a. Linear0
    b. Thing
    c. Undefined
    d. Undefined

128. A _____ is a first degree polynomial mathematical function of the form: f(x) = mx + b where m and b are real constants and x is a real variable.
    a. Thing
    b. Linear function0
    c. Undefined
    d. Undefined

129. _____ is a method of building database-backed software applications.
    a. Scaffolding0
    b. Thing
    c. Undefined
    d. Undefined

130. In physics, a _____ may refer to the scalar _____ or to the vector _____.
    a. Potential0
    b. Thing
    c. Undefined
    d. Undefined

131. In mathematical analysis, _____ are objects which generalize functions and probability distributions.
    a. Thing
    b. Distribution0
    c. Undefined
    d. Undefined

132. _____ (Groups, Algorithms and Programming) is a computer algebra system for computational discrete algebra with particular emphasis on, but not restricted to, computational group theory.
    a. Gap0
    b. Thing
    c. Undefined
    d. Undefined

133. The _____ of an object is the extra energy which it possesses due to its motion.

Chapter 8. USING THE DEFINITE INTEGRAL

    a. Thing
    c. Undefined
    b. Kinetic energy0
    d. Undefined

134. In physics, the _____ momentum of an object rotating about some reference point is the measure of the extent to which the object will continue to rotate about that point unless acted upon by an external torque.
    a. Thing
    c. Undefined
    b. Angular0
    d. Undefined

135. In physics, the _____ is a vector quantity (more precisely, a pseudovector) which specifies the angular speed at which an object is rotating along with the direction in which it is rotating.
    a. Angular velocity0
    c. Undefined
    b. Thing
    d. Undefined

136. _____ is the middle point of a line segment.
    a. Midpoint0
    c. Undefined
    b. Thing
    d. Undefined

137. _____ measures the nominal future sum of money that a given sum of money is "worth" at a specified time in the future assuming a certain interest rate; this value does not include corrections for inflation or other factors that affect the true value of money in the future.
    a. Future value0
    c. Undefined
    b. Thing
    d. Undefined

138. _____ of a single or multiple future payments is the nominal amounts of money to change hands at some future date, discounted to account for the time value of money, and other factors such as investment risk.
    a. Thing
    c. Undefined
    b. Present value0
    d. Undefined

139. The _____ is a popular form of gambling which involves the drawing of lots for a prize. Some governments forbid it, while others endorse it to the extent of organizign a national _____
    a. Lottery0
    c. Undefined
    b. Thing
    d. Undefined

140. A _____ function is a function for which, intuitively, small changes in the input result in small changes in the output.
    a. Event
    c. Undefined
    b. Continuous0
    d. Undefined

141. _____ is a regular and continuing flow of money generated by a business or investment
    a. Thing
    c. Undefined
    b. Income stream0
    d. Undefined

142. _____ is a business term for the amount of money that a company receives from its activities in a given period, mostly from sales of products and/or services to customers

Chapter 8. USING THE DEFINITE INTEGRAL

a. Thing
b. Revenue0
c. Undefined
d. Undefined

143. In mathematics, _____ is the decomposition of an object into a product of other objects, or factors, which when multiplied together give the original.
a. Thing
b. Factoring0
c. Undefined
d. Undefined

144. _____ is the fee paid on borrowed money.
a. Interest0
b. Thing
c. Undefined
d. Undefined

145. An _____ is the fee paid on borrow money.
a. Concept
b. Interest rate0
c. Undefined
d. Undefined

146. In economics, _____ describe market relations between prospective sellers and buyers of a good.
a. Supply and demand0
b. Thing
c. Undefined
d. Undefined

147. _____ can be defined as the graph depicting the relationship between the price of a certain commodity, and the amount of it that consumers are willing and able to purchase at that given price demand.
a. Thing
b. Demand curve0
c. Undefined
d. Undefined

148. A _____ is an individual or household that purchases and uses goods and services generated within the economy.
a. Consumer0
b. Thing
c. Undefined
d. Undefined

149. In economics, economic _____ is simply a state of the world where economic forces are balanced and in the absence of external influences the values of economic variables will not change.
a. Thing
b. Equilibrium0
c. Undefined
d. Undefined

150. _____ is the price at which the quantity demanded of a good or service is equal to the quantity supplied.
a. Thing
b. Equilibrium price0
c. Undefined
d. Undefined

151. _____ is used in economics for several related quantities
a. Producer surplus0
b. Thing
c. Undefined
d. Undefined

152. A _____ is a deliberate process for transforming one or more inputs into one or more results.

Chapter 8. USING THE DEFINITE INTEGRAL

    a. Thing
    b. Calculation0
    c. Undefined
    d. Undefined

153. _____ finance, in finance, a debt security, issued by Issuer
    a. Bond0
    b. Thing
    c. Undefined
    d. Undefined

154. In set theory and other branches of mathematics, the _____ of a collection of sets is the set that contains everything that belongs to any of the sets, but nothing else.
    a. Union0
    b. Thing
    c. Undefined
    d. Undefined

155. A _____ is a type of debt. All material things can be lent but this article focuses exclusively on monetary loans. Like all debt instruments, a _____ entails the redistribution of financial assets over time, between the lender and the borrower.
    a. Thing
    b. Loan0
    c. Undefined
    d. Undefined

156. Deductive _____ is the kind of _____ in which the conclusion is necessitated by, or reached from, previously known facts (the premises).
    a. Reasoning0
    b. Thing
    c. Undefined
    d. Undefined

157. In statistics, a _____ is a graphical display of tabulated frequencies.
    a. Histogram0
    b. Concept
    c. Undefined
    d. Undefined

158. In statistics the _____ of an event i is the number n_i of times the event occurred in the experiment or the study. These frequencies are often graphically represented in histograms.
    a. Frequency0
    b. Concept
    c. Undefined
    d. Undefined

159. A _____ is a function for which, intuitively, small changes in the input result in small changes in the output.
    a. Event
    b. Continuous function0
    c. Undefined
    d. Undefined

160. _____ is a synonym for information.
    a. Thing
    b. Data0
    c. Undefined
    d. Undefined

161. The _____ integers are all the integers from zero on upwards.
    a. Thing
    b. Nonnegative0
    c. Undefined
    d. Undefined

162. _____ Any process by which a specified characteristic usually amplitude of the output of a device is prevented from exceeding a predetermined value.

Chapter 8. USING THE DEFINITE INTEGRAL

a. Thing
b. Limiting0
c. Undefined
d. Undefined

163. In set theory and its applications throughout mathematics, _____ are a collection of sets (or sometimes other mathematical objects) that can be unambiguously defined by a property that all its members share.
a. Classes0
b. Thing
c. Undefined
d. Undefined

164. In the scientific method, an _____ (Latin: ex-+-periri, "of (or from) trying"), is a set of actions and observations, performed in the context of solving a particular problem or question, in order to support or falsify a hypothesis or research concerning phenomena.
a. Thing
b. Experiment0
c. Undefined
d. Undefined

165. _____ are a measure of time.
a. Thing
b. Minutes0
c. Undefined
d. Undefined

166. The _____ of a geographic location is its height above a fixed reference point, often the mean sea level.
a. Thing
b. Elevation0
c. Undefined
d. Undefined

167. _____ is the chance that something is likely to happen or be the case.
a. Probability0
b. Thing
c. Undefined
d. Undefined

168. In mathematics, the _____ of a function is the set of all "output" values produced by that function. Given a function $f : A \to B$, the _____ of f, is defined to be the set $\{x \in B : x = f(a) \text{ for some } a \in A\}$.
a. Thing
b. Range0
c. Undefined
d. Undefined

169. In mathematics, an _____, mean, or central tendency of a data set refers to a measure of the "middle" or "expected" value of the data set.
a. Concept
b. Average0
c. Undefined
d. Undefined

170. The _____, the average in everyday English, which is also called the arithmetic _____ (and is distinguished from the geometric _____ or harmonic _____). The average is also called the sample _____. The expected value of a random variable, which is also called the population _____.
a. Thing
b. Mean0
c. Undefined
d. Undefined

171. In probability theory and statistics, a _____ is a number dividing the higher half of a sample, a population, or a probability distribution from the lower half.

Chapter 8. USING THE DEFINITE INTEGRAL

    a. Median0   b. Concept
    c. Undefined   d. Undefined

172. In mathematics, science including computer science, linguistics and engineering, an _____ is, generally speaking, an independent variable or input to a function.
    a. Thing   b. Argument0
    c. Undefined   d. Undefined

173. An _____ is the limit of a definite integral, as an endpoint of the interval of integration approaches either a specified real number or ‡ or − ‡ or, in some cases, as both endpoints approach limits.
    a. Improper integral0   b. Thing
    c. Undefined   d. Undefined

174. The _____, also called Gaussian distribution by scientists, is a continuous probability distribution of great importance in many fields.
    a. Thing   b. Normal distribution0
    c. Undefined   d. Undefined

175. _____, also called Gaussian distribution by scientists, is a continuous probability distribution of great importance in many fields.
    a. Normal distributions0   b. Thing
    c. Undefined   d. Undefined

176. _____ of a probability distribution, random variable, or population or multiset of values is a measure of the spread of its values.
    a. Standard deviation0   b. Thing
    c. Undefined   d. Undefined

177. _____ is a measure of difference for interval and ratio variables between the observed value and the mean.
    a. Deviation0   b. Thing
    c. Undefined   d. Undefined

178. _____ is an adjective usually refering to being in the centre.
    a. Thing   b. Central0
    c. Undefined   d. Undefined

179. _____ is a trigonemtric function that is important when studying triangles and modeling periodic phenomena, among other applications.
    a. Sine0   b. Thing
    c. Undefined   d. Undefined

180. In mathematics, the _____ is a conic section generated by the intersection of a right circular conical surface and a plane parallel to a generating straight line of that surface. It can also be defined as locus of points in a plane which are equidistant from a given point.

Chapter 8. USING THE DEFINITE INTEGRAL

a. Parabola0
b. Thing
c. Undefined
d. Undefined

181. _____ is a three-dimensional geometric shape formed by straight lines through a fixed point vertex to the points of a fixed curve directrix.
   a. Thing
   b. Right circular cone0
   c. Undefined
   d. Undefined

182. In geometry, a _____ is a surface of revolution generated by revolving a circle in three dimensional space about an axis coplanar with the circle, which does not touch the circle. Examples of tori include the surfaces of doughnuts and inner tubes. A circle rotated about a chord of the circle is called a _____ in some contexts, but this is not a common usage in mathematics. The shape produced when a circle is rotated about a chord resembles a round cushion. _____ was the Latin word for a cushion of this shape.
   a. Torus0
   b. Thing
   c. Undefined
   d. Undefined

183. _____, from Latin meaning "to make progress", is defined in two different ways. Pure economic _____ is the increase in wealth that an investor has from making an investment, taking into consideration all costs associated with that investment including the opportunity cost of capital.
   a. Profit0
   b. Thing
   c. Undefined
   d. Undefined

184. In mathematics, a _____ of a number x is a number r such that $r^2 = x$, or in words, a number r whose square (the result of multiplying the number by itself) is x.
   a. Square root0
   b. Thing
   c. Undefined
   d. Undefined

185. In mathematics, a _____ of a complex-valued function f is a member x of the domain of f such that f(x) vanishes at x, that is, $x : f(x) = 0$.
   a. Root0
   b. Thing
   c. Undefined
   d. Undefined

186. U.S. liquid _____ is legally defined as 231 cubic inches, and is equal to 3.785411784 litres or abotu 0.13368 cubic feet. This is the most common definition of a _____. The U.S. fluid ounce is defined as 1/128 of a U.S. _____.
   a. Gallon0
   b. Thing
   c. Undefined
   d. Undefined

187. _____ is a branch of mathematics concerning the study of structure, relation and quantity.
   a. Algebra0
   b. Concept
   c. Undefined
   d. Undefined

188. In mathematics, the _____ functions are functions of an angle; they are important when studying triangles and modeling periodic phenomena, among many other applications.

Chapter 8. USING THE DEFINITE INTEGRAL

   a. Trigonometric0
   c. Undefined
   b. Thing
   d. Undefined

189. An _____ is an equality that remains true regardless of the values of any variables that appear within it, to distinguish it from an equality which is true under more particular conditions.
   a. Identity0
   c. Undefined
   b. Thing
   d. Undefined

190. _____ is a function that represents a probability distribution in terms of integrals.
   a. Probability density function0
   c. Undefined
   b. Thing
   d. Undefined

191. In common philosophical language, a proposition or _____, is the content of an assertion, that is, it is true-or-false and defined by the meaning of a particular piece of language.
   a. Statement0
   c. Undefined
   b. Concept
   d. Undefined

192. The _____ is a measurement of how a function changes when the values of its inputs change.
   a. Derivative0
   c. Undefined
   b. Thing
   d. Undefined

193. A _____ is a three-dimensional solid object bounded by six square faces, facets, or sides, with three meeting at each vertex.
   a. Cube0
   c. Undefined
   b. Thing
   d. Undefined

194. An _____ of a product of sums expresses it as a sum of products by using the fact that multiplication distributes over addition.
   a. Thing
   c. Undefined
   b. Expansion0
   d. Undefined

195. _____ is the state of being greater than any finite real or natural number, however large.
   a. Infinite0
   c. Undefined
   b. Thing
   d. Undefined

196. In mathematics, a set is called _____ if there is a bijection between the set and some set of the form {1, 2, ..., n} where n is a natural number.
   a. Finite0
   c. Undefined
   b. Thing
   d. Undefined

197. A _____ is the sum of the elements of a sequence.
   a. Thing
   c. Undefined
   b. Series0
   d. Undefined

198. _____ denotes the approach toward a definite value, as time goes on; or to a definite point, a common view or opinion, or toward a fixed or equilibrium state.

Chapter 8. USING THE DEFINITE INTEGRAL

a. Convergence0
c. Undefined
b. Thing
d. Undefined

199. Acid _____ ratio measures the ability of a company to use its near cash or quick assets to immediately extinguish its current liabilities.
   a. Thing
   b. Test0
   c. Undefined
   d. Undefined

200. _____ in one variable is an infinite series of the form
   a. Power series0
   b. Thing
   c. Undefined
   d. Undefined

Chapter 9. SEQUENCES AND SERIES

1. In mathematics, a _____ is an ordered list of objects. Like a set, it contains members, also called elements or terms, and the number of terms is called the length of the _____. Unlike a set, order matters, and the exact same elements can appear multiple times at different positions in the _____.
   - a. Sequence0
   - b. Thing
   - c. Undefined
   - d. Undefined

2. A _____ is the sum of the elements of a sequence.
   - a. Series0
   - b. Thing
   - c. Undefined
   - d. Undefined

3. _____ is the state of being greater than any finite real or natural number, however large.
   - a. Thing
   - b. Infinite0
   - c. Undefined
   - d. Undefined

4. A _____ is a negotiable instrument instructing a financial institution to pay a specific amount of a specific currency from a specific demand account held in the maker/depositor's name with that institution. Both the maker and payee may be natural persons or legal entities.
   - a. Thing
   - b. Check0
   - c. Undefined
   - d. Undefined

5. _____ has many meanings, most of which simply .
   - a. Thing
   - b. Power0
   - c. Undefined
   - d. Undefined

6. A _____ is a numeral used to indicate a count. The most common use of the word today is to name the part of a fraction that tells the number or count of equal parts.
   - a. Numerator0
   - b. Thing
   - c. Undefined
   - d. Undefined

7. _____ is often used to describe the measurement of the steepness, incline, gradient, or grade of a straight line. The _____ is defined as the ratio of the "rise" divided by the "run" between two points on a line, or in other words, the ratio of the altitude change to the horizontal distance between any two points on the line.
   - a. Thing
   - b. Slope0
   - c. Undefined
   - d. Undefined

8. The word _____ comes from the Latin word linearis, which means created by lines.
   - a. Linear0
   - b. Thing
   - c. Undefined
   - d. Undefined

9. A _____ is a first degree polynomial mathematical function of the form: f(x) = mx + b where m and b are real constants and x is a real variable.
   - a. Linear function0
   - b. Thing
   - c. Undefined
   - d. Undefined

10. A _____ is the part of a fraction that tells how many equal parts make up a whole, and which is used in the name of the fraction: "halves", "thirds", "fourths" or "quarters", "fifths" and so on.

Chapter 9. SEQUENCES AND SERIES

    a. Concept
    b. Denominator0
    c. Undefined
    d. Undefined

11. The mathematical concept of a _____ expresses the intuitive idea of deterministic dependence between two quantities, one of which is viewed as primary and the other as secondary. A _____ then is a way to associate a unique output for each input of a specified type, for example, a real number or an element of a given set.
    a. Thing
    b. Function0
    c. Undefined
    d. Undefined

12. An _____ is a straight line around which a geometric figure can be rotated.
    a. Axis0
    b. Thing
    c. Undefined
    d. Undefined

13. In astronomy, geography, geometry and related sciences and contexts, a plane is said to be _____ at a given point if it is locally perpendicular to the gradient of the gravity field, i.e., with the direction of the gravitational force at that point.
    a. Horizontal0
    b. Thing
    c. Undefined
    d. Undefined

14. A _____ is a one-dimensional picture in which the integers are shown as specially-marked points evenly spaced on a line.
    a. Number line0
    b. Thing
    c. Undefined
    d. Undefined

15. In mathematics, when a method of defining functions is utilized, in which the function being defined is applied within its own definition, that pertaining function is called _____.
    a. Thing
    b. Recursive0
    c. Undefined
    d. Undefined

16. In plane geometry, a _____ is a polygon with four equal sides, four right angles, and parallel opposite sides. In algebra, the _____ of a number is that number multiplied by itself.
    a. Square0
    b. Thing
    c. Undefined
    d. Undefined

17. The _____ are the only integral domain whose positive elements are well-ordered, and in which order is preserved by addition. Like the natural numbers, the _____ form a countably infinite set. The set of all _____ is usually denoted in mathematics by a boldface Z .
    a. Thing
    b. Integers0
    c. Undefined
    d. Undefined

18. _____ means in succession or back-to-back
    a. Thing
    b. Consecutive0
    c. Undefined
    d. Undefined

19. A _____ is traditionally an infinitesimally small change in a variable.

a. Differential0   b. Thing
c. Undefined   d. Undefined

20. A _____ is a mathematical equation for an unknown function of one or several variables which relates the values of the function itself and of its derivatives of various orders.
   a. Thing   b. Differential equation0
   c. Undefined   d. Undefined

21. A _____ signifies a point or points of probability on a subject e.g., the _____ of creativity, which allows for the formation of rule or norm or law by interpretation of the phenomena events that can be created.
   a. Principle0   b. Thing
   c. Undefined   d. Undefined

22. _____ is a method of mathematical proof typically used to establish that a given statement is true of all natural numbers
   a. Mathematical induction0   b. Thing
   c. Undefined   d. Undefined

23. _____ denotes the approach toward a definite value, as time goes on; or to a definite point, a common view or opinion, or toward a fixed or equilibrium state.
   a. Thing   b. Convergence0
   c. Undefined   d. Undefined

24. In mathematical analysis and related areas of mathematics, a set is called _____, if it is, in a certain sense, of finite size.
   a. Thing   b. Bounded0
   c. Undefined   d. Undefined

25. In mathematics, _____ describes an entity with a limit.
   a. Convergent0   b. Thing
   c. Undefined   d. Undefined

26. In mathematics, a _____ is a statement that can be proved on the basis of explicitly stated or previously agreed assumptions.
   a. Thing   b. Theorem0
   c. Undefined   d. Undefined

27. In mathematics, a _____ is a demonstration that, assuming certain axioms, some statement is necessarily true.
   a. Thing   b. Proof0
   c. Undefined   d. Undefined

28. _____ are the basic objects of study in graph theory. Informally speaking, a graph is a set of objects called points, nodes, or vertices connected by links called lines or edges.
   a. Graphs0   b. Thing
   c. Undefined   d. Undefined

Chapter 9. SEQUENCES AND SERIES

29. _____ is the design, analysis, and/or construction of works for practical purposes.
    a. Thing
    b. Engineering0
    c. Undefined
    d. Undefined

30. A _____ function is a function for which, intuitively, small changes in the input result in small changes in the output.
    a. Continuous0
    b. Event
    c. Undefined
    d. Undefined

31. _____ is a subset of a population.
    a. Sample0
    b. Thing
    c. Undefined
    d. Undefined

32. _____ is the part of statistical practice concerned with the selection of individual observations intended to yield some knowledge about a population of concern, especially for the purposes of statistical inference.
    a. Thing
    b. Sampling0
    c. Undefined
    d. Undefined

33. In mathematics, an _____, mean, or central tendency of a data set refers to a measure of the "middle" or "expected" value of the data set.
    a. Average0
    b. Concept
    c. Undefined
    d. Undefined

34. A _____ is a type of debt. All material things can be lent but this article focuses exclusively on monetary loans. Like all debt instruments, a _____ entails the redistribution of financial assets over time, between the lender and the borrower.
    a. Loan0
    b. Thing
    c. Undefined
    d. Undefined

35. _____ is the fee paid on borrowed money.
    a. Thing
    b. Interest0
    c. Undefined
    d. Undefined

36. _____ is a kind of property which exists as magnitude or multitude. It is among the basic classes of things along with quality, substance, change, and relation.
    a. Amount0
    b. Thing
    c. Undefined
    d. Undefined

37. _____ is a physical property of a system that underlies the common notions of hot and cold; something that is hotter has the greater _____.
    a. Temperature0
    b. Thing
    c. Undefined
    d. Undefined

38. A _____ is a quantity that denotes the proportional amount or magnitude of one quantity relative to another.

a. Ratio0
b. Thing
c. Undefined
d. Undefined

39. _____ is a term used in accounting, economics and finance with reference to the fact that assets with finite lives lose value over time.
a. Depreciation0
b. Thing
c. Undefined
d. Undefined

40. A _____ is one of the basic shapes of geometry: a polygon with three vertices and three sides which are straight line segments.
a. Triangle0
b. Thing
c. Undefined
d. Undefined

41. Leonardo of Pisa (1170s or 1180s – 1250), also known as Leonardo Pisano, Leonardo Bonacci, Leonardo _____, or, most commonly, simply _____, was an Italian mathematician, considered by some "the most talented mathematician of the Middle Ages."
a. Person
b. Fibonacci0
c. Undefined
d. Undefined

42. In mathematics and the mathematical sciences, a _____ is a fixed, but possibly unspecified, value. This is in contrast to a variable, which is not fixed.
a. Thing
b. Constant0
c. Undefined
d. Undefined

43. A _____ of a number is the product of that number with any integer.
a. Thing
b. Multiple0
c. Undefined
d. Undefined

44. A _____ is the result of the addition of a set of numbers. The numbers may be natural numbers, complex numbers, matrices, or still more complicated objects. An infinite _____ is a subtle procedure known as a series.
a. Sum0
b. Thing
c. Undefined
d. Undefined

45. In mathematics, a set is called _____ if there is a bijection between the set and some set of the form {1, 2, ..., n} where n is a natural number.
a. Finite0
b. Thing
c. Undefined
d. Undefined

46. The _____ of a mathematical object is its size: a property by which it can be larger or smaller than other objects of the same kind; in technical terms, an ordering of the class of objects to which it belongs.
a. Thing
b. Magnitude0
c. Undefined
d. Undefined

47. In banking and accountancy, the outstanding _____ is the amount of money owned, or due, that remains in a deposit account or a loan account at a given date, after all past remittances, payments and withdrawal have been accounted for.

Chapter 9. SEQUENCES AND SERIES

   a. Thing
   b. Balance0
   c. Undefined
   d. Undefined

48. In mathematics, the multiplicative inverse of a number x, denoted 1/x or x^{-1}, is the number which, when multiplied by x, yields 1. The multiplicative inverse of x is also called the _____ of x.
   a. Reciprocal0
   b. Thing
   c. Undefined
   d. Undefined

49. An _____ is a combination of numbers, operators, grouping symbols and/or free variables and bound variables arranged in a meaningful way which can be evaluated..
   a. Expression0
   b. Thing
   c. Undefined
   d. Undefined

50. A _____ is a deliberate process for transforming one or more inputs into one or more results.
   a. Thing
   b. Calculation0
   c. Undefined
   d. Undefined

51. A _____ is a special kind of ratio, indicating a relationship between two measurements with different units, such as miles to gallons or cents to pounds.
   a. Thing
   b. Rate0
   c. Undefined
   d. Undefined

52. An _____ is the fee paid on borrow money.
   a. Concept
   b. Interest rate0
   c. Undefined
   d. Undefined

53. The act of _____ is the calculated approximation of a result which is usable even if input data may be incomplete, uncertain, or noisy.
   a. Estimating0
   b. Thing
   c. Undefined
   d. Undefined

54. In geometry, a _____ is defined as a quadrilateral where all four of its angles are right angles.
   a. Thing
   b. Rectangle0
   c. Undefined
   d. Undefined

55. Mathematical _____ are demonstrations that,assuming certain axioms, some statement is necessarily true.
   a. Thing
   b. Proofs0
   c. Undefined
   d. Undefined

56. An _____ is the limit of a definite integral, as an endpoint of the interval of integration approaches either a specified real number or ‡ or − ‡ or, in some cases, as both endpoints approach limits.
   a. Thing
   b. Improper integral0
   c. Undefined
   d. Undefined

57. The _____ of a function is an extension of the concept of a sum, and are identified or found through the use of integration.

Chapter 9. SEQUENCES AND SERIES

    a. Integral0
    c. Undefined
    b. Thing
    d. Undefined

58. In acoustics and telecommunication, the _____ of a wave is a component frequency of the signal that is an integer multiple of the fundamental frequency.
    a. Thing
    c. Undefined
    b. Harmonic0
    d. Undefined

59. _____ is often represented as the sum of a sequence of terms.
    a. Infinite series0
    c. Undefined
    b. Thing
    d. Undefined

60. The _____, the average in everyday English, which is also called the arithmetic _____ (and is distinguished from the geometric _____ or harmonic _____). The average is also called the sample _____. The expected value of a random variable, which is also called the population _____.
    a. Mean0
    c. Undefined
    b. Thing
    d. Undefined

61. In mathematics, the concept of a _____ tries to capture the intuitive idea of a geometrical one-dimensional and continuous object. A simple example is the circle.
    a. Curve0
    c. Undefined
    b. Thing
    d. Undefined

62. _____ is a method used to test infinite series of non-negative terms for convergence.
    a. Thing
    c. Undefined
    b. Integral Test0
    d. Undefined

63. Acid _____ ratio measures the ability of a company to use its near cash or quick assets to immediately extinguish its current liabilities.
    a. Thing
    c. Undefined
    b. Test0
    d. Undefined

64. The term _____ is defined dually as an element of P which is lesser than or equal to every element of S.
    a. Lower bound0
    c. Undefined
    b. Thing
    d. Undefined

65. In mathematics, especially in order theory, an _____ of a subset S of some partially ordered set is an element of P which is greater than or equal to every element of S.
    a. Upper bound0
    c. Undefined
    b. Thing
    d. Undefined

66. In mathematics, a _____ series is an infinite series that is not convergent, meaning that the infinite sequence of the partial sums of the series does not have a limit.
    a. Divergent0
    c. Undefined
    b. Thing
    d. Undefined

Chapter 9. SEQUENCES AND SERIES

67. _____ is an infinite series that is not convergent, meaning that the infinite sequence of the partial sums of the series does not have a limit.
    a. Thing
    b. Divergent series0
    c. Undefined
    d. Undefined

68. _____ is a criterion for convergence or divergence of a series whose terms are real or complex numbers.
    a. Thing
    b. Comparison test0
    c. Undefined
    d. Undefined

69. _____ is electromagnetic radiation with a wavelength that is visible to the eye (visible _____) or, in a technical or scientific context, electromagnetic radiation of any wavelength.
    a. Light0
    b. Thing
    c. Undefined
    d. Undefined

70. _____ is an operator that measures the magnitude of a vector field's source or sink at a given point; the _____ of a vector field is a signed scalar.
    a. Thing
    b. Divergence0
    c. Undefined
    d. Undefined

71. A _____ is a statement or claimt that a particular event will occur in the future in more certain terms than a forecast.
    a. Prediction0
    b. Thing
    c. Undefined
    d. Undefined

72. In mathematics, the _____ (or modulus) of a real number is its numerical value without regard to its sign.
    a. Thing
    b. Absolute value0
    c. Undefined
    d. Undefined

73. _____ is a test or "criterion" for the convergence of a series
    a. Thing
    b. Ratio Test0
    c. Undefined
    d. Undefined

74. _____ is an infinite series of the form
    a. Thing
    b. Alternating series0
    c. Undefined
    d. Undefined

75. A _____ consists either of a suggested explanation for a phenomenon or of a reasoned proposal suggesting a possible correlation between multiple phenomena.
    a. Hypothesis0
    b. Thing
    c. Undefined
    d. Undefined

76. The material _____, also known as the material implication or truth functional _____, expresses a property of certain conditionals in logic.
    a. Thing
    b. Conditional0
    c. Undefined
    d. Undefined

77. _____ a series is the sum of the terms of a sequence of numbers.
   a. Thing
   b. Convergent series0
   c. Undefined
   d. Undefined

78. In common philosophical language, a proposition or _____, is the content of an assertion, that is, it is true-or-false and defined by the meaning of a particular piece of language.
   a. Statement0
   b. Concept
   c. Undefined
   d. Undefined

79. _____ is a method used to prove that infinite series of terms converge.
   a. Alternating series test0
   b. Thing
   c. Undefined
   d. Undefined

80. _____ in one variable is an infinite series of the form
   a. Power series0
   b. Thing
   c. Undefined
   d. Undefined

81. In elementary algebra, an _____ is a set that contains every real number between two indicated numbers and may contain the two numbers themselves.
   a. Thing
   b. Interval0
   c. Undefined
   d. Undefined

82. In mathematics, a _____ of a complex-valued function f is a member x of the domain of f such that f(x) vanishes at x, that is, x : f (x) = 0.
   a. Root0
   b. Thing
   c. Undefined
   d. Undefined

83. _____ is a criterion for the convergence of an infinite series
   a. Root Test0
   b. Thing
   c. Undefined
   d. Undefined

84. In mathematics, an inequality is a statement about the relative size or order of two objects. For example 14 > 10, or 14 is _____ 10.
   a. Greater than0
   b. Thing
   c. Undefined
   d. Undefined

85. Mathematical _____ is used to represent ideas.
   a. Thing
   b. Notation0
   c. Undefined
   d. Undefined

86. In geometry, an _____ is a point at which a line segment or ray terminates.
   a. Thing
   b. Endpoint0
   c. Undefined
   d. Undefined

Chapter 9. SEQUENCES AND SERIES

87. In classical geometry, a _____ of a circle or sphere is any line segment from its center to its boundary. By extension, the _____ of a circle or sphere is the length of any such segment. The _____ is half the diameter. In science and engineering the term _____ of curvature is commonly used as a synonym for _____.
   a. Radius0
   b. Thing
   c. Undefined
   d. Undefined

88. In mathematics, a _____ is a constant multiplicative factor of a certain object. The object can be such things as a variable, a vector, a function, etc. For example, the _____ of $9x^2$ is 9.
   a. Coefficient0
   b. Thing
   c. Undefined
   d. Undefined

89. In elementary algebra, a _____ is a polynomial with two terms: the sum of two monomials. It is the simplest kind of polynomial except for a monomial.
   a. Binomial0
   b. Thing
   c. Undefined
   d. Undefined

90. _____ first defined by the mathematician Daniel Bernoulli and generalized by Friedrich Bessel, are canonical solutions y(x) of Bessel's differential equation:
   a. Thing
   b. Bessel function0
   c. Undefined
   d. Undefined

91. Kepler's laws of _____ are his primary contributions to astronomy/astrophysics. Kepler, a German mathematician, studied the observations of the legendarily precise Danish astronomer Tycho Brahe, and found around 1605 that these observations followed three relatively simple mathematical laws.
   a. Planetary motion0
   b. Thing
   c. Undefined
   d. Undefined

92. In mathematics, a _____ of a k-place relation $L \subseteq X_1 \times ... \times X_k$ is one of the sets X_j, $1 \leq j \leq k$. In the special case where k = 2 and $L \subseteq X_1 \times X_2$ is a function $L : X_1 \rightarrow X_2$, it is conventional to refer to X_1 as the _____ of the function and to refer to X_2 as the codomain of the function.
   a. Domain0
   b. Thing
   c. Undefined
   d. Undefined

93. In mathematics, a _____ is an expression that is constructed from one or more variables and constants, using only the operations of addition, subtraction, multiplication, and constant positive whole number exponents. is a _____. Note in particular that division by an expression containing a variable is not in general allowed in polynomials. [1]
   a. Thing
   b. Polynomial0
   c. Undefined
   d. Undefined

94. The _____ is a measurement of how a function changes when the values of its inputs change.
   a. Thing
   b. Derivative0
   c. Undefined
   d. Undefined

95. In mathematics, _____ is an elementary arithmetic operation. When one of the numbers is a whole number, _____ is the repeated sum of the other number.

Chapter 9. SEQUENCES AND SERIES

a. Multiplication0
b. Thing
c. Undefined
d. Undefined

96. The deductive-nomological model is a formalized view of scientific _____ in natural language.
   a. Thing
   b. Explanation0
   c. Undefined
   d. Undefined

97. _____ finance, in finance, a debt security, issued by Issuer
   a. Thing
   b. Bond0
   c. Undefined
   d. Undefined

98. _____ Logic is a concept in traditional logic referring to a "type of immediate inference in which from a given proposition another proposition is inferred which has as its subject the predicate of the original proposition and as its predicate the subject of the original proposition (the quality of the proposition being retained)."
   a. Concept
   b. Converse0
   c. Undefined
   d. Undefined

99. The _____ integers are all the integers from zero on upwards.
   a. Nonnegative0
   b. Thing
   c. Undefined
   d. Undefined

100. In mathematics, an _____ is a statement about the relative size or order of two objects.
   a. Inequality0
   b. Thing
   c. Undefined
   d. Undefined

101. _____ is the chance that something is likely to happen or be the case.
   a. Probability0
   b. Thing
   c. Undefined
   d. Undefined

102. _____ are activities that are governed by a set of rules or customs and often engaged in competitively.
   a. Sports0
   b. Thing
   c. Undefined
   d. Undefined

103. A _____ is 360° or 2∂ radians.
   a. Thing
   b. Turn0
   c. Undefined
   d. Undefined

104. The population _____ is the total number of human beings alive on the planet Earth at a given time.
   a. Thing
   b. Of the world0
   c. Undefined
   d. Undefined

105. In mathematics, the additive inverse, or _____ of a number n is the number that, when added to n, yields zero. The additive inverse of n is denoted −n. For example, 7 is −7, because 7 + (−7) = 0, and the additive inverse of −0.3 is 0.3, because −0.3 + 0.3 = 0.

Chapter 9. SEQUENCES AND SERIES

a. Opposite0
b. Thing
c. Undefined
d. Undefined

106. In mathematics, the _____ of a number n is the number that, when added to n, yields zero. The _____ of n is denoted −n. For example, 7 is −7, because 7 + (−7) = 0, and the _____ of −0.3 is 0.3, because −0.3 + 0.3 = 0.
   a. Thing
   b. Additive inverse0
   c. Undefined
   d. Undefined

107. _____ is a trigonemtric function that is important when studying triangles and modeling periodic phenomena, among other applications.
   a. Thing
   b. Sine0
   c. Undefined
   d. Undefined

108. The _____ of an angle is the ratio of the length of the adjacent side to the length of the hypotenuse.
   a. Cosine0
   b. Concept
   c. Undefined
   d. Undefined

109. A _____ is a function that repeats its values after some definite period has been added to its independent variable.
   a. Thing
   b. Periodic function0
   c. Undefined
   d. Undefined

Chapter 10. APPROXIMATING FUNCTIONS USING SERIES

1. A _____ is an undefined term. However, it is often thought of as a series of points. A _____ has one dimension - length. A _____ is either named by a lower case letter or by two points on the _____.
   a. Line10
   b. 15 theorem
   c. Undefined
   d. Undefined

2. The word _____ can have three meanings: In _____ theory, a _____ is an abstract object consisting of vertices (or nodes) and edges (or arcs) between pairs of vertices. The _____ of a function f : X ¨ Y is the set of all pairs (x,f(x)) The _____ of a relation, a generalisation of the _____ of a function.
   a. Graph10
   b. 15 theorem
   c. Undefined
   d. Undefined

3. A <U>point </U>is an undefined term. We usually represent this by a dot, but a _____ actually has no dimension. A capital letter names any _____.
   a. Point10
   b. 15 theorem
   c. Undefined
   d. Undefined

4. A _____ is a class of simple functions where they are constructed using only multiplication and addition of terms.
   a. Polynomial10
   b. 15 theorem
   c. Undefined
   d. Undefined

5. A _____ is a number or variable, or the product or quotient of a number or variable.
   a. Term10
   b. 15 theorem
   c. Undefined
   d. Undefined

6. A number that does not change in value in a given situation is a _____.
   a. Constant10
   b. 15 theorem
   c. Undefined
   d. Undefined

7. The probability of correctly rejecting a false Ho is referred to as _____.
   a. Power10
   b. 15 theorem
   c. Undefined
   d. Undefined

8. In a large distribution of data it is often easier to understand the data if it is grouped into intervals where each _____ can contain more than one data value. Distributions are often reduced to 10 to 20 intervals.
   a. ACTRAN
   b. Interval10
   c. Undefined
   d. Undefined

9. The <U>radius</U> of a circle is the distance from the center to the circle.
   a. Radius10
   b. 15 theorem
   c. Undefined
   d. Undefined

10. A _____ is simply a polynomial with two terms such as this example: 2x + 7.
    a. 15 theorem
    b. Binomial10
    c. Undefined
    d. Undefined

Chapter 10. APPROXIMATING FUNCTIONS USING SERIES

11. A _____ is a multiplicative factor of a certain object such as a variable (for example, the coefficients of a polynomial), a basis vector, a basis function and so on. Usually, the objects and the coefficients are indexed in the same way, leading to expressions such as $a_1x_1 + a_2x_2 + a_3x_3 + ...$ where a_n is the _____ of the variable x_n for each $n = 1, 2, 3, ...$
    a. Coefficient10
    b. 15 theorem
    c. Undefined
    d. Undefined

12. _____ is used synonymously for variable.
    a. 15 theorem
    b. Factor10
    c. Undefined
    d. Undefined

13. An _____ combines numbers, operators, and/or variables but contains no equal or inequality sign.
    a. Expression10
    b. ACTRAN
    c. Undefined
    d. Undefined

14. The very fact that we are measuring objects with respect to some characteristic implies that the objects differ in that characteristic; or stated in another way, that the characteristic can take on a number of different values. These properties or characteristics of an object that can assume two or more different values are referred to as a _____.
    a. Variable10
    b. 15 theorem
    c. Undefined
    d. Undefined

15. A <U>quadratic</U> contains at least one squared term.
    a. Quadratic10
    b. 15 theorem
    c. Undefined
    d. Undefined

16. The <U>opposite </U>of a number is the number that makes a sum zero. In most cases, this means just to change the sign. 3 is the _____ of -3.
    a. Opposite10
    b. ACTRAN
    c. Undefined
    d. Undefined

17. There are properties of objects that do assume one and only value, and we refer to these characteristics as _____. _____, then, are the invariables that differentiate one class of objects from another.
    a. 15 theorem
    b. Constants10
    c. Undefined
    d. Undefined

18. An <U>equation</U> is represented by two expressions that have the same value.
    a. Equation10
    b. ACTRAN
    c. Undefined
    d. Undefined

19. When a value makes an equation true, it is called a <U>solution</U>. 3 is a _____ of $x + 2 = 5$,
    a. Solution10
    b. 15 theorem
    c. Undefined
    d. Undefined

20. An _____ is an indication of the value of an unknown quantity based on observed data. More formally, an _____ is the particular value of an estimator that is obtained from a particular sample of data and used to indicate the value of a parameter.

a. Estimate10   b. ACTRAN
c. Undefined   d. Undefined

21. A quadrilateral with 4 equal sides and all right angles is called a <U>square.</U>
a. Square10   b. 15 theorem
c. Undefined   d. Undefined

22. _____ consist of the positive natural numbers (1, 2, 3, ...), their negatives (−1, −2, −3, ...) and the number zero.
a. Integers10   b. ACTRAN
c. Undefined   d. Undefined

23. Addition (or summation) is one of the basic operations of arithmetic. In its simplest form, addition combines two numbers, the augend and addend, into a single number, the _____. Adding more numbers can be viewed as repeated addition. (Repeated addition of the number one is the most basic form of counting.) By extension, the addition of zero numbers, one number, or infinitely many numbers can be defined.
a. Sum10   b. 15 theorem
c. Undefined   d. Undefined

24. A _____ is a quotient of numbers, like 3/4, or more generally, an element of a quotient field.
a. 15 theorem   b. Fraction10
c. Undefined   d. Undefined

25. The _____ or central tendency of a list of n numbers. The most common method, and the one generally referred to simply as the _____, is the arithmetic mean.
a. ACTRAN   b. Average10
c. Undefined   d. Undefined

26. By _____ we mean collecting observations made upon our environment -- observations, which are the results of measurements using clocks, balances, measuring rods, counting operations, or other objectively defined measuring instruments or procedures. _____ may mean simply counting the number of times a particular property occurs.
a. 15 theorem   b. Data10
c. Undefined   d. Undefined

27. _____ is a central branch of mathematics, developed from algebra and geometry, and built on two major complementary ideas, differential _____ and integral _____.
a. 15 theorem   b. Calculus10
c. Undefined   d. Undefined

28. The point of intersection of the horizontal and vertical axes in the rectangular coordinate plane is the _____. It is is expressed as the ordered pair (0,0).
a. Origin10   b. ACTRAN
c. Undefined   d. Undefined

29. The answer to subtraction is called the <U>difference</U>.

Chapter 10. APPROXIMATING FUNCTIONS USING SERIES

a. Difference10
c. Undefined
b. 15 theorem
d. Undefined

30. A _____ is the relationship between two quantities. It is expressed as the quotient of two numbers, or as two numbers separated by a colon (pronounced "to"). A number that can be written as a _____ of two integers is a rational number.

a. Ratio10
c. Undefined
b. 15 theorem
d. Undefined

31. _____, or less commonly, denary, usually refers to the base 10 numeral system.

a. Decimal10
c. Undefined
b. 15 theorem
d. Undefined

Chapter 11. DIFFERENTIAL EQUATIONS

1. An <U>equation</U> is represented by two expressions that have the same value.
    a. ACTRAN
    b. Equation11
    c. Undefined
    d. Undefined

2. When a value makes an equation true, it is called a <U>solution</U>. 3 is a _____ of x + 2 = 5,
    a. Solution11
    b. 15 theorem
    c. Undefined
    d. Undefined

3. There are properties of objects that do assume one and only value, and we refer to these characteristics as _____. _____, then, are the invariables that differentiate one class of objects from another.
    a. Constants11
    b. 15 theorem
    c. Undefined
    d. Undefined

4. A number that does not change in value in a given situation is a _____.
    a. 15 theorem
    b. Constant11
    c. Undefined
    d. Undefined

5. A _____ is an undefined term. However, it is often thought of as a series of points. A _____ has one dimension - length. A _____ is either named by a lower case letter or by two points on the _____.
    a. Line11
    b. 15 theorem
    c. Undefined
    d. Undefined

6. The _____ refers to the amount of change in Y for a 1 unit change in X or is the ratio of the rise over the run; or in-other-words, the rate of change in the predicted value as a function of a change in the predictor variable.
    a. 15 theorem
    b. Slope11
    c. Undefined
    d. Undefined

7. A <U>line segment </U>is a piece of a line. The _____ has definite length and is named by the two endpoints.
    a. Line segment11
    b. 15 theorem
    c. Undefined
    d. Undefined

8. The point of intersection of the horizontal and vertical axes in the rectangular coordinate plane is the _____. It is is expressed as the ordered pair (0,0).
    a. Origin11
    b. ACTRAN
    c. Undefined
    d. Undefined

9. Whenever you divide by zero the answer is <U>undefined.</U>
    a. ACTRAN
    b. Undefined11
    c. Undefined
    d. Undefined

10. A <U>point </U>is an undefined term. We usually represent this by a dot, but a _____ actually has no dimension. A capital letter names any _____.
    a. 15 theorem
    b. Point11
    c. Undefined
    d. Undefined

11. A <U>plane</U> is an undefined term. We can think of it as a series of lines having 2 dimensions, width and length.

Chapter 11. DIFFERENTIAL EQUATIONS

a. Plane11
b. 15 theorem
c. Undefined
d. Undefined

12. A _____ is a well-defined collection of objects considered as a whole.
   a. Set11
   b. 15 theorem
   c. Undefined
   d. Undefined

13. _____ are characteristics or properties of an object that can take on one or more different values.
   a. Variables11
   b. 15 theorem
   c. Undefined
   d. Undefined

14. A _____, also referred to as a universe, is any well-defined collection of things. By well-defined we mean that the members of the _____ are spelled out, or an unequivocal statement is made as to which things belong in it and which do not.
   a. Population11
   b. 15 theorem
   c. Undefined
   d. Undefined

15. A percentage is a way of expressing a proportion, a ratio or a fraction as a whole number, by using 100 as the denominator. A number such as "45%" ("45 percent" or "45 per cent") is shorthand for the fraction 45/100 or 0.45.As an illustration,"45 _____ of human beings..." is equivalent to both of the following:"45 out of every 100 people..." "0.45 of the human population..." One way to think about percentages is to realize that "one percent", represented by the symbol %, is simply the number 1/100, or 0.01.
   a. Percent11
   b. 15 theorem
   c. Undefined
   d. Undefined

16. The word _____ can have three meanings: In _____ theory, a _____ is an abstract object consisting of vertices (or nodes) and edges (or arcs) between pairs of vertices. The _____ of a function f : X ¨ Y is the set of all pairs (x,f(x)) The _____ of a relation, a generalisation of the _____ of a function.
   a. 15 theorem
   b. Graph11
   c. Undefined
   d. Undefined

17. At times we must contend with variables that assume a large number of values. In this case it is typical to create _____ of values of the variable and then make a frequency tally of the number of observations falling within each interval. As is the case with any data reduction technique, detail is lost.
   a. Intervals11
   b. ACTRAN
   c. Undefined
   d. Undefined

18. The answer to subtraction is called the <U>difference</U>.
   a. Difference11
   b. 15 theorem
   c. Undefined
   d. Undefined

19. _____ is the change in x between two points
   a. Run11
   b. 15 theorem
   c. Undefined
   d. Undefined

20. _____ refer to any data source, whether individuals, physical or biological things, geographic locations, time periods, or events; that is, anything upon which observations can be made.
   a. ACTRAN
   b. Objects11
   c. Undefined
   d. Undefined

21. _____, or less commonly, denary, usually refers to the base 10 numeral system.
   a. 15 theorem
   b. Decimal11
   c. Undefined
   d. Undefined

22. Horizontal axis of display containing the trailing digits is called _____.
   a. 15 theorem
   b. Leaves11
   c. Undefined
   d. Undefined

23. An _____ is an indication of the value of an unknown quantity based on observed data. More formally, an _____ is the particular value of an estimator that is obtained from a particular sample of data and used to indicate the value of a parameter.
   a. Estimate11
   b. ACTRAN
   c. Undefined
   d. Undefined

24. The probability of correctly rejecting a false Ho is referred to as _____.
   a. Power11
   b. 15 theorem
   c. Undefined
   d. Undefined

25. By _____ we mean the cumulative frequency, counting in from the nearer end.
   a. Depth11
   b. 15 theorem
   c. Undefined
   d. Undefined

26. A _____ is a multiplicative factor of a certain object such as a variable (for example, the coefficients of a polynomial), a basis vector, a basis function and so on. Usually, the objects and the coefficients are indexed in the same way, leading to expressions such as $a_1x_1 + a_2x_2 + a_3x_3 + ...$ where an is the _____ of the variable xn for each n = 1, 2, 3, ...
   a. Coefficient11
   b. 15 theorem
   c. Undefined
   d. Undefined

27. _____ is used synonymously for variable.
   a. 15 theorem
   b. Factor11
   c. Undefined
   d. Undefined

28. Any time one number is on the left side of another number on a number line, the first number is <U>less than </U>the second number. The symbol for this is <.
   a. 15 theorem
   b. Less than11
   c. Undefined
   d. Undefined

29. An _____ combines numbers, operators, and/or variables but contains no equal or inequality sign.

Chapter 11. DIFFERENTIAL EQUATIONS

    a. Expression11   b. ACTRAN
    c. Undefined   d. Undefined

30. Addition (or summation) is one of the basic operations of arithmetic. In its simplest form, addition combines two numbers, the augend and addend, into a single number, the _____. Adding more numbers can be viewed as repeated addition. (Repeated addition of the number one is the most basic form of counting.) By extension, the addition of zero numbers, one number, or infinitely many numbers can be defined.
    a. Sum11   b. 15 theorem
    c. Undefined   d. Undefined

31. A _____ is a quotient of numbers, like 3⁄4, or more generally, an element of a quotient field.
    a. 15 theorem   b. Fraction11
    c. Undefined   d. Undefined

32. The <U>radius</U> of a circle is the distance from the center to the circle.
    a. Radius11   b. 15 theorem
    c. Undefined   d. Undefined

33. In inferential statistics where we are using a statistic to infer differences we need at least two different variables typically called an _____ and a dependent variable. The _____ represents the variable of interest, that is, the variable in which an inference is being made as to whether categories of that variable should be considered the same or different. There must be at least two categories or groupings for this variable in order to make comparisons. The variable is said to be independent since the categories are arbitrarily assigned by the investigator.
    a. Independent variable11   b. ACTRAN
    c. Undefined   d. Undefined

34. By _____ we mean collecting observations made upon our environment -- observations, which are the results of measurements using clocks, balances, measuring rods, counting operations, or other objectively defined measuring instruments or procedures. _____ may mean simply counting the number of times a particular property occurs.
    a. 15 theorem   b. Data11
    c. Undefined   d. Undefined

35. A _____ is a mathematical function when plotted on an x,y graph forms a straight line.
    a. 15 theorem   b. Linear function11
    c. Undefined   d. Undefined

36. A _____ is the result of multiplying, or an expression that identifies factors to be multiplied
    a. 15 theorem   b. Product11
    c. Undefined   d. Undefined

37. The number of times a particular score or observation occurs is its _____.
    a. Frequency11   b. 15 theorem
    c. Undefined   d. Undefined

38. If one number is to the right of another number on the number line, this number is <U>greater than </U>the number on the left. The symbol that is used is >.

Chapter 11. DIFFERENTIAL EQUATIONS

a. 15 theorem
b. Greater than11
c. Undefined
d. Undefined

39. In a factorial design with two or more main effects or grouping effects, there is a possibility of a significant _____ effect, AB. With a significant _____ you have differences in estimates of the population variance in the various combinations, or cells, of one main effect paired with another. Interactions must be explained before main effects in a statistical analysis. The _____ is tested using an F test in an ANOVA that compares the MSab/Mserror.
   a. ACTRAN
   b. Interaction11
   c. Undefined
   d. Undefined

40. A quadrilateral with 4 equal sides and all right angles is called a <U>square.</U>
   a. 15 theorem
   b. Square11
   c. Undefined
   d. Undefined

41. An _____ is any process or study, which results in the collection of data, the outcome of which is unknown. In statistics, the term is usually restricted to situations in which the researcher has control over some of the conditions under which the _____ takes place.
   a. Experiment11
   b. ACTRAN
   c. Undefined
   d. Undefined

42. The defining characteristics of populations are called _____. Observations must be made on every single member of the population in question in order to precisely state the value of _____.
   a. Parameters11
   b. 15 theorem
   c. Undefined
   d. Undefined

43. <U>Twice</U> means to multiply by 2.
   a. Twice11
   b. 15 theorem
   c. Undefined
   d. Undefined

44. The <U>opposite </U>of a number is the number that makes a sum zero. In most cases, this means just to change the sign. 3 is the _____ of -3.
   a. ACTRAN
   b. Opposite11
   c. Undefined
   d. Undefined

45. A _____ is a number or variable, or the product or quotient of a number or variable.
   a. Term11
   b. 15 theorem
   c. Undefined
   d. Undefined

46. A <U>quadratic</U> contains at least one squared term.
   a. 15 theorem
   b. Quadratic11
   c. Undefined
   d. Undefined

47. An _____ is the result of an experiment or other situation involving uncertainty.
   a. Outcome11
   b. ACTRAN
   c. Undefined
   d. Undefined

Chapter 11. DIFFERENTIAL EQUATIONS

48. _____ (or summation) is one of the basic operations of arithmetic. In its simplest form, _____ combines two numbers, the augend and addend, into a single number, the sum.
   a. Addition11
   b. ACTRAN
   c. Undefined
   d. Undefined

49. _____ is a branch of mathematics which studies structure and quantity. It may be roughly characterized as a generalization and abstraction of arithmetic, in which operations are performed on symbols rather than numbers. It includes elementary _____, taught to high school students, as well as abstract _____ which covers such structures as groups, rings and fields. Along with geometry and analysis, it is one of the three principal branches of mathematics.
   a. ACTRAN
   b. Algebra11
   c. Undefined
   d. Undefined

Chapter 1

1. a	2. a	3. a	4. a	5. a	6. a	7. a	8. b	9. b	10. b
11. b	12. b	13. b	14. a	15. b	16. a	17. b	18. a	19. b	20. a
21. a	22. a	23. b	24. b	25. b	26. a	27. a	28. b	29. b	30. b
31. b	32. a	33. a	34. a	35. b	36. a	37. b	38. b	39. a	40. b
41. a	42. a	43. a	44. a	45. b	46. a	47. a	48. b	49. a	50. b
51. b	52. a	53. b	54. a	55. b	56. b	57. b	58. a	59. b	60. b
61. b	62. b	63. a	64. a	65. a	66. a	67. b	68. a	69. b	70. b
71. b	72. a	73. b	74. b	75. a	76. a	77. b	78. a	79. a	80. b
81. a	82. a	83. b	84. a	85. b	86. a	87. a	88. b	89. a	90. b
91. a	92. b	93. b	94. a	95. b	96. a	97. a	98. a	99. a	100. a
101. a	102. b	103. a	104. a	105. a	106. a	107. a	108. b	109. a	110. b
111. b	112. b	113. b	114. a	115. a	116. a	117. b	118. b	119. b	120. a
121. a	122. b	123. a	124. b	125. b	126. b	127. a	128. b	129. b	130. a
131. b	132. a	133. b	134. a	135. b	136. a	137. a	138. b	139. a	140. b
141. b	142. b	143. b	144. a	145. a	146. a	147. b	148. b	149. a	150. b
151. b	152. a	153. a	154. b	155. b	156. b	157. b	158. a	159. a	160. b
161. a	162. b	163. a	164. b	165. a	166. b	167. b	168. b	169. a	170. b
171. b	172. a	173. a	174. b						

Chapter 2

1. b	2. a	3. a	4. b	5. a	6. b	7. b	8. b	9. b	10. b
11. a	12. b	13. b	14. b	15. a	16. b	17. a	18. a	19. b	20. b
21. b	22. b	23. b	24. b	25. a	26. b	27. a	28. a	29. a	30. a
31. b	32. b	33. a	34. b	35. b	36. b	37. b	38. b	39. b	40. b
41. a	42. b	43. a	44. a	45. b	46. a	47. a	48. b	49. a	50. a
51. a	52. a	53. b	54. a	55. a	56. a	57. b	58. a	59. a	60. a
61. a	62. a	63. b	64. a	65. a	66. a	67. a	68. b	69. b	70. a
71. a	72. a	73. b	74. b	75. a	76. a	77. a	78. a	79. a	80. a
81. a	82. b	83. b	84. a	85. b	86. b	87. a	88. a	89. a	90. b
91. a	92. b	93. a	94. a	95. b	96. b	97. b	98. b	99. a	100. a
101. a	102. a	103. a	104. b						

Chapter 3

1. a	2. b	3. a	4. a	5. b	6. a	7. a	8. b	9. b	10. a
11. b	12. b	13. a	14. a	15. a	16. b	17. b	18. b	19. b	20. b
21. b	22. b	23. a	24. a	25. a	26. a	27. a	28. a	29. a	30. b
31. a	32. a	33. a	34. b	35. b	36. a	37. a	38. a	39. b	40. a
41. a	42. b	43. b	44. b	45. b	46. a	47. a	48. b	49. a	50. b
51. b	52. a	53. b	54. b	55. b	56. b	57. a	58. a	59. b	60. b
61. b	62. a	63. b	64. a	65. a	66. b	67. a	68. a	69. b	70. b
71. b	72. a	73. b	74. b	75. a	76. a	77. a	78. b	79. a	80. a
81. b	82. a	83. a	84. b	85. a	86. a	87. a	88. a	89. a	90. a
91. b	92. a	93. b	94. b	95. a	96. b	97. a	98. b	99. b	100. a
101. b	102. b	103. b	104. a	105. a	106. b	107. b	108. b	109. a	110. b
111. b	112. a	113. a	114. a	115. a	116. b	117. b	118. a	119. b	120. b
121. a	122. b	123. b	124. a	125. a	126. a				

ANSWER KEY

Chapter 4

1. b	2. a	3. b	4. a	5. b	6. b	7. b	8. a	9. b	10. b
11. b	12. b	13. b	14. b	15. a	16. a	17. b	18. b	19. a	20. b
21. a	22. a	23. a	24. b	25. a	26. b	27. b	28. a	29. b	30. a
31. a	32. b	33. a	34. b	35. a	36. a	37. b	38. b	39. b	40. a
41. b	42. b	43. b	44. a	45. b	46. b	47. a	48. a	49. b	50. b
51. a	52. b	53. b	54. b	55. b	56. b	57. b	58. b	59. b	60. b
61. b	62. b	63. b	64. b	65. a	66. a	67. b	68. b	69. a	70. b
71. a	72. a	73. b	74. a	75. b	76. b	77. b	78. a	79. b	80. a
81. b	82. a	83. b	84. a	85. b	86. b	87. b	88. b	89. a	90. b
91. a	92. b	93. b	94. a	95. a	96. b	97. a	98. a	99. b	100. a
101. b	102. a	103. a	104. b	105. a	106. b	107. a	108. b	109. a	110. b
111. a	112. b	113. b	114. b	115. b	116. b	117. a	118. b	119. b	120. a
121. a	122. a	123. a	124. b	125. b	126. b	127. b	128. a	129. b	130. a
131. b	132. b	133. a	134. a	135. b	136. a	137. a	138. a	139. b	140. a
141. b	142. a	143. a	144. b	145. a	146. a	147. a	148. a	149. b	150. b
151. a	152. b	153. b	154. a	155. b	156. b	157. b	158. b	159. a	160. b
161. b	162. a	163. a	164. a	165. b	166. b	167. b	168. b	169. a	170. b
171. b	172. b	173. a	174. a	175. b	176. b	177. b	178. a	179. b	180. a
181. a	182. b	183. b	184. a	185. b	186. a	187. a	188. b	189. a	190. b
191. a	192. a	193. b	194. a						

Chapter 5

1. b	2. b	3. a	4. b	5. b	6. a	7. b	8. b	9. a	10. a
11. a	12. b	13. a	14. a	15. a	16. a	17. a	18. a	19. a	20. b
21. b	22. b	23. a	24. a	25. b	26. b	27. b	28. a	29. a	30. a
31. a	32. b	33. a	34. a	35. b	36. b	37. b	38. a	39. a	40. a
41. a	42. a	43. a	44. a	45. a	46. b	47. b	48. b	49. b	50. a
51. a	52. b	53. a	54. a	55. b	56. a	57. a	58. a	59. a	60. b
61. b	62. a	63. b	64. a	65. b	66. b	67. b	68. b	69. b	70. a
71. a	72. a	73. a	74. b	75. a	76. b	77. b	78. b	79. b	80. a
81. b	82. a	83. b	84. a	85. b	86. b	87. b	88. a	89. b	90. b
91. a	92. a								

Chapter 6

1. a	2. a	3. b	4. a	5. a	6. b	7. a	8. a	9. b	10. a
11. a	12. a	13. a	14. b	15. a	16. b	17. a	18. a	19. b	20. a
21. a	22. b	23. a	24. a	25. a	26. b	27. a	28. b	29. a	30. b
31. a	32. b	33. b	34. a	35. b	36. a	37. a	38. b	39. b	40. a
41. b	42. a	43. a	44. a	45. b	46. a	47. b	48. b	49. b	50. b
51. b	52. b	53. a	54. a	55. a	56. b	57. a	58. b	59. a	60. b
61. b	62. a	63. a	64. b	65. b	66. b	67. b	68. b	69. a	70. b
71. b	72. b	73. b	74. b	75. b	76. a	77. a	78. a	79. a	80. a
81. b	82. b	83. a	84. a	85. a	86. b	87. a	88. b	89. b	90. a
91. b	92. b	93. b	94. a	95. b	96. b	97. b	98. b	99. b	100. b
101. b	102. a								

Chapter 7

1. a	2. b	3. b	4. b	5. b	6. a	7. b	8. a	9. a	10. a
11. a	12. a	13. a	14. b	15. b	16. b	17. b	18. b	19. b	20. a
21. b	22. b	23. b	24. a	25. a	26. b	27. a	28. b	29. a	30. b
31. a	32. a	33. a	34. a	35. b	36. a	37. a	38. a	39. a	40. a
41. a	42. b	43. a	44. a	45. b	46. a	47. b	48. b	49. a	50. b
51. b	52. b	53. a	54. b	55. b	56. a	57. b	58. a	59. b	60. a
61. b	62. b	63. a	64. b	65. b	66. b	67. b	68. a	69. a	70. a
71. a	72. a	73. a	74. b	75. a	76. a	77. b	78. a	79. b	80. a
81. b	82. a	83. b	84. b	85. b	86. b	87. a	88. b	89. a	90. b
91. a	92. b	93. a	94. b	95. b	96. a	97. b	98. b	99. a	100. b
101. a	102. b	103. a	104. a	105. a	106. b	107. b	108. b	109. a	110. b
111. a	112. a	113. a	114. a	115. a	116. a	117. a	118. b	119. b	120. b
121. a	122. a	123. b	124. a	125. b	126. a	127. a	128. b	129. a	130. b
131. b	132. b	133. b	134. b	135. a	136. b	137. b	138. a	139. a	140. b
141. a	142. b	143. b	144. a	145. b					

ANSWER KEY

Chapter 8

1. a	2. a	3. a	4. a	5. b	6. a	7. b	8. b	9. a	10. a
11. b	12. a	13. a	14. a	15. a	16. a	17. b	18. a	19. a	20. a
21. b	22. b	23. b	24. b	25. b	26. b	27. b	28. a	29. b	30. b
31. b	32. b	33. b	34. a	35. b	36. a	37. b	38. a	39. b	40. b
41. b	42. b	43. b	44. b	45. a	46. a	47. a	48. a	49. b	50. a
51. b	52. b	53. b	54. b	55. a	56. a	57. a	58. b	59. b	60. a
61. a	62. a	63. b	64. b	65. b	66. b	67. b	68. b	69. a	70. b
71. b	72. b	73. b	74. b	75. b	76. a	77. a	78. a	79. b	80. a
81. a	82. b	83. b	84. a	85. b	86. b	87. b	88. a	89. b	90. a
91. b	92. a	93. b	94. a	95. a	96. b	97. a	98. a	99. a	100. b
101. a	102. b	103. a	104. b	105. b	106. a	107. b	108. b	109. b	110. a
111. a	112. b	113. b	114. a	115. a	116. a	117. b	118. b	119. a	120. b
121. a	122. b	123. b	124. a	125. a	126. a	127. a	128. b	129. a	130. a
131. b	132. a	133. b	134. b	135. a	136. a	137. a	138. b	139. a	140. b
141. b	142. b	143. b	144. a	145. b	146. a	147. b	148. a	149. b	150. b
151. a	152. b	153. a	154. a	155. b	156. a	157. a	158. a	159. b	160. b
161. b	162. b	163. a	164. b	165. b	166. b	167. a	168. b	169. b	170. b
171. a	172. b	173. a	174. b	175. a	176. b	177. a	178. b	179. a	180. a
181. b	182. a	183. a	184. a	185. a	186. a	187. a	188. a	189. a	190. a
191. a	192. a	193. a	194. b	195. a	196. a	197. b	198. a	199. b	200. a

Chapter 9

1. a	2. a	3. b	4. b	5. b	6. a	7. b	8. a	9. a	10. b
11. b	12. a	13. a	14. a	15. b	16. a	17. b	18. b	19. a	20. b
21. a	22. a	23. b	24. b	25. a	26. b	27. b	28. a	29. b	30. a
31. a	32. b	33. a	34. a	35. b	36. a	37. a	38. a	39. a	40. a
41. b	42. b	43. b	44. a	45. a	46. b	47. b	48. a	49. a	50. b
51. b	52. b	53. a	54. b	55. b	56. b	57. a	58. b	59. a	60. a
61. a	62. b	63. b	64. a	65. a	66. a	67. b	68. b	69. a	70. b
71. a	72. b	73. b	74. b	75. a	76. b	77. b	78. a	79. a	80. a
81. b	82. a	83. a	84. a	85. b	86. b	87. a	88. a	89. a	90. b
91. a	92. a	93. b	94. b	95. a	96. b	97. b	98. b	99. a	100. a
101. a	102. a	103. b	104. b	105. a	106. b	107. b	108. a	109. b	

Chapter 10

1. a	2. a	3. a	4. a	5. a	6. a	7. a	8. b	9. a	10. b
11. a	12. b	13. a	14. a	15. a	16. a	17. b	18. a	19. a	20. a
21. a	22. a	23. a	24. b	25. b	26. b	27. b	28. a	29. a	30. a
31. a									

Chapter 11

1. b	2. a	3. a	4. b	5. a	6. b	7. a	8. a	9. b	10. b
11. a	12. a	13. a	14. a	15. a	16. b	17. a	18. a	19. a	20. b
21. b	22. b	23. a	24. a	25. a	26. a	27. b	28. b	29. a	30. a
31. b	32. a	33. a	34. b	35. b	36. b	37. a	38. b	39. b	40. b
41. a	42. a	43. a	44. b	45. a	46. b	47. a	48. a	49. b	

www.ingramcontent.com/pod-product-compliance
Lightning Source LLC
Chambersburg PA
CBHW082205230426
43672CB00015B/2911